Praise for previous editions of

Wedding Toasts Made Easy

"Author Tom Haibeck's book, 'Wedding Toasts Made Easy' got the ultimate plug when Regis Philbin featured it on his show and talked about how much it helped him in preparing a toast for his daughter's wedding."

HOSEA SANDERS
ABC-7 News Chicago

"It's a great book covering one of the most difficult parts of a wedding. I highly recommend it to anyone faced with having to speak at a wedding reception."

RICHARD MARKEL
President, Association for Wedding Professionals International

"I'm telling you – a lot of people are going to want to buy this book! What a great idea for the best man or anyone else in the wedding party that has to make a speech."

MARIANNE McCLARY
Good Day Sacramento

"Remember it's not a roast or bachelor party. Keep it clean! says Tom Haibeck, author of Wedding Toasts Made Easy!"

MALEGRAMS
Men's Health Magazine

"As a wedding planner, I can tell you that the quality and timing of the toasts at a wedding can make an enormous difference. I recommend "Wedding Toasts Made Easy" to all my clients.

ELAINE PARKER
Weddings With Elan, Nashville, Tennessee

"It covers everything they need to know about how to write and propose a compelling toast. As a matter of fact, I sent both my sons a copy when they were married and the book helped ensure that each of their weddings was a great success."

LINDA REDMOND
Associate Publisher, Wedding Bells Magazine

"Thanks for doing such a great job and helping brides, grooms, best men and fathers everywhere!"

RANDY BARTLETT
Premier Entertainment, Sacramento, California

"Consider what you would want people to say about you and your spouse if it were your wedding, says Tom Haibeck, author of Wedding Toasts Made Easy."

ALISON WINN SCOTCH
Hallmark Magazine

Wedding Toasts Made Easy

The Complete Guide

Written by Tom Haibeck
Illustrations by Grahame Arnould

First printing in April, 1990
Reprinted in October, 1993
Reprinted in December, 1998
Reprinted in April, 2000
Reprinted in November, 2002
Reprinted in May, 2004
Reprinted in March, 2005
U.S. edition: Printed in March, 2005
Revised and reprinted in May, 2006
Revised and reprinted in August, 2009

Library of Congress Control Number: 2005922668

Haibeck, Tom, 1957-
Wedding toasts made easy : the complete guide
/ Tom Haibeck – Rev. ed.

ISBN: 978-0-9697051-6-1

1. Wedding etiquette. 2. Weddings–Planning. 3. Masters of ceremonies. I. Title.

BJ2065.M37H35 2009   395.2'2   C2009-903616-9

Printed and bound in the United States of America
by United Graphics, Incorporated
Mattoon, Illinois

Cover Design: Foster Covers
Photos: Kent Kallberg Photography
Cartoons: Grahame Arnould
Typesetting: Typewise Design Studio

Published by:
The Haibeck Communications Group Inc.

Telephone: (604) 671-5491
E-Mail: tom@haibeck.com

WeddingToasts.com

*This book is dedicated to the
joy of a wedding – and to all the people
who contribute to that special day.*

Contents

Foreword

Weddings are my business. For nearly 20 years, I have helped plan and have provided entertainment services for hundreds of wedding receptions in Southern California and across America.

During that time, I have seen my share of wedding reception disasters. From drunken speeches and inappropriate toasts to out-of-control guests who have turned an otherwise beautiful wedding into a free-for-all, I know firsthand just how devastating those kinds of experiences can be for the bride and groom and for their families.

The toasts and speeches at a wedding can often set the tone for the entire evening. If they're in poor taste or made with little advance preparation, the entire wedding reception can be negatively affected. On the other hand, if the speakers are well-prepared and know what they are doing, the wedding speeches and toasts can help set the stage for an entertaining, festive wedding reception.

That's why I am happy to recommend *"Wedding Toasts Made Easy."* The advice offered in the book is invaluable for anyone asked to speak at a wedding – and it's presented in a humorous, easy-to-read fashion that's concise and to the point.

I consider it "must read" material for anyone given the honor of offering a wedding toast.

— **PETER MERRY, PRESIDENT**
American Disc Jockey Association
Merry Weddings, Los Angeles, CA

*"Good evening, everyone. I'm the Uncle of the Bride.
Can you believe she actually agreed to marry this bum?"*

An Introduction To This Book

It happens every weekend in ballrooms, meeting halls and other special event venues around the world. Someone stands to offer a wedding toast – and falls flat on their face in the process.

It might be a wedding speech that runs on far too long, a drunken diatribe about the groom's past life "back at the frat house" or a deadly dull attempt at being funny or profound. Alternatively, it could be a lip quivering, shaken-to-the-core performance by some unfortunate soul who is terrified of public speaking (and that includes many of us).

This book has been written to help people avoid those kinds of nightmares. If you've purchased it – or someone else has bought it for you – you're probably either:

a) someone who has been asked to make a toast
   at an upcoming wedding reception;

b) one of the key decision-makers in the planning
   of the wedding (the bride, groom or their parents)
   who wants to help ensure that the toasts at the
   wedding are a hit;

c) a professional who has been asked to help plan
   and organize the event (a wedding planner,
   disc jockey or master of ceremonies).

No matter which category you fall into, I think you will find this book helpful. Because by taking the time to read it, you will be better prepared than 99% of the people who get married, plan weddings or make toasts. And the net result will make an enormous difference at the wedding.

You see, one of the most memorable parts of nearly every wedding is the reception party that follows. And the most memorable element of that reception is often the wedding speeches and toasts that are at the center of it.

Guests don't necessarily remember precisely what people said; but they will remember being entertained, being moved to laughter or tears, and feeling like the wedding reception was fun and enjoyable.

On the other hand, a wedding reception can be remembered for all the wrong reasons. We've all been to weddings that were dull, disorganized and even disastrous. And we've all witnessed wedding speakers that were unprepared, drunk and obnoxious.

WHY I WROTE THIS BOOK

Those kinds of experiences can be incredibly embarrassing for the couple and their families (I know that from personal experience). My goal in writing this book is to help you avoid those kinds of disasters – whether you're making a toast, emceeing the wedding or getting married.

In the pages that follow, you will very quickly learn what it takes to put together an outstanding wedding toast. This newly-expanded edition also includes tips for the person chosen to emcee the wedding (whether it's a professional DJ, a close friend or a member of the family). By the way, the international version of this book, *"The Wedding MC: A Complete Guide to Success for the Master of Ceremonies"* is available at **TheWeddingMCBook.com**.

The advice I offer is based on my 25+ years in writing speeches and providing speaker training for corporate executives; my own experience as a speaker and emcee; and my background in public relations, broadcasting and event management. It's concise, humorous and easy to read. And it's been endorsed by wedding professionals and event planners all over the world.

The balance of this book is directed towards helping people asked to make a wedding toast succeed in doing so. And as you're about to discover, my first experience in that role quite literally left me (and a few other people) speechless.

SPEECHLESS ON LONG ISLAND

I made my first wedding toast at the age of 15. My older brother had asked me to be the best man at his wedding, and I felt pretty special being asked. I had no idea what a "best man" actually does at a wedding, but I knew it was a big deal and that it would involve getting a new suit.

The wedding was to take place later that year in New York. That was a long way from home – and as it turned out, more than a few zip codes out of my comfort zone.

My family was from a small town out west, and none of us (other than my brother and my dad) had ever been to New York before – let alone to a high society wedding. But that was the scene that was about to unfold, as the bride-to-be was the eldest daughter of a prominent family from New York (no, not the Sopranos).

She and my brother had met through a mutual friend while attending college. For reasons that are still unclear to me, she actually fell for him and accepted his offer of marriage.

JUST ANOTHER GALA EVENT ON MY CALENDAR

The wedding was to take place in the backyard of her parents' home on Long Island. They were quite wealthy, and as you can imagine, it was destined to be a rather gala affair. It would also be the first wedding for our family – and the first one that I had ever attended.

Fortunately, I had no idea at the time that my participation would involve making a toast. For had I known that when my brother asked me to be his best man, I probably would have declined. Frankly, I had a phobia about speaking in public – and like most 15-year-olds, had never made a toast in my life (in fact, I don't think I even knew what a "wedding toast" was).

A few weeks prior to the wedding, somebody mentionied that the best man was expected to make a toast. I began to panic, and thought seriously about telling my brother to choose someone else. But given the short notice (and out of respect to him), I decided to wing it. Besides, I didn't want to have to return that fancy new suit or miss out on the trip to New York.

In the days leading up to the wedding, I began to imagine all sorts of catastrophes. I had no idea what to say or how to say it – and the thought of having to stand up in front of all those people was about the worst thing I could imagine.

THE UNABASHED STARS OF SHOW & TELL

It wasn't always like that for me. Way back in Grade One, I could hardly wait to take my turn at "show and tell." Speaking up in class was just a natural thing to do – we didn't think much about it, we just did it – and had fun doing so!

But something happened during the process of going through those early school years that ate away at my confidence in addressing an audience. And frankly, I think that's a very common experience for people growing up.

Maybe it's the awkwardness we begin to experience in entering adolescence. Or the self-consciousness that often plagues teenagers. Whatever the reason, many of us seem to lose our childhood bravado and develop a fear of public speaking that can plague us for life.

So there I was on the day of the wedding, a kid from the prairies about to be thrust centre stage before the blue bloods of Long Island. It's early June, with the temperature in the 90's and the air so thick I can barely breathe.

A TIE THAT COMES WITH A CLIP

I'm wandering around the assembled throng with a frozen grin on my face, trying to appear grown-up and sophisticated in my fancy new suit. But my clip-on tie has imprisoned me, and I've never felt this kind of heat and humidity. I'm soaked in sweat and starting to feel nauseous, knowing that some 150 guests are soon going to be staring at me when I offer my little tribute to the bride and groom.

My older sister spots me and tells me "it's time." She nudges me forward into the centre of the patio. It's packed with blue-haired ladies and cigar-smoking men in tuxedos. They're all drinking, laughing and enjoying themselves. The noise is deafening, as everyone seems to be talking at once. No one takes any notice of my sister and me – and I'm thinking that's good, maybe they'll cancel the toast. But before I can slink into the background, my sister starts banging a spoon against her glass.

AND NOW IT'S TIME FOR TOM'S TOAST!
Suddenly, the party comes to a dead halt. Conversations stop. Heads turn from every direction. A thousand eyeballs are suddenly focussed on me, the clammy kid in the two-toned sweat suit. I'm shaking inside and wondering why I ever agreed to do this.

My sister stops ringing her glass and asks for everyone's attention. She then introduces me as the best man, and tells everyone that I would like to make a toast. A polite smattering of applause ensues.

I look back at the crowd. I look up at the sky. I look down at the deck. I begin to wonder if I remembered to do up my fly.

My sister glares at me. I feel like I'm going to faint. Or throw-up. Or both. If there is, in fact, a hell, I'm in the center of it.

I look over at my brother and his new bride. They sense my panic, and are now silently willing me to speak, nodding their heads as if to say "You can do this." The hush remains. People start to fidget. The deadly silence gives way to a low murmur.

TO JOHN AND WHAT'S HER NAME
My mind is racing – I can't remember what I was going to say. My face is growing hotter and I can feel that dull little pain that begins to grow in the back of my throat when I'm about to cry.

I take a sip of my ginger ale to try to wash it away. It's still there. My entire body is trembling and I feel like I might hurl any second on my shiny new loafers. Funny, but I don't remember feeling this way back at show and tell.

I open my mouth to speak. My voice quivers. I know this has to be quick. *"To John and uh ...."* (I've now forgotten the name of my new sister-in-law). Through clenched teeth, my sister hisses: *"Jill!"* Right. *"To John and Jill!"*

MORE JAM WITH HER TOAST

It's all I can muster, the little speech I had tried so hard to memorize for the occasion proves completely unattainable. I immediately take a big glug of my ginger ale, thinking that will signal the audience to join me in the toast. But no one seems to know what to do. Finally, my sister shouts out, *"To John and Jill!"* and the audience chimes in with raised glasses.

The party resumes, and my new sister-in-law comes forward to give me a little hug. I can tell she's disappointed – it's not quite the tribute she'd envisioned. My brother shakes my hand and rolls his eyes. I start to breathe again. And mercifully – it's over.

I can laugh about it now, but at the time, it was an incredibly traumatic experience (as it would be for most 15-year-olds). I was quite literally a basket case – scared to death of speaking in public, clueless about what to say or how to say it, and no one to coach me through the exercise.

So here's the good news: Having seen just how hard it was for me to make that toast, my dad decided to do something for me that completely changed my life. He enrolled me in a public speaking program (The Dale Carnegie Course). Through that, I was able to overcome my fear of public speaking – and the confidence I gained in doing so extended into every area of my life. When you conquer your fear of public speaking, you can do anything.

BRINGING DOWN THE HOUSE

Over the years, I've heard similar stories from hundreds of readers (and many of the clients I have personally coached). They've read this book, done what I've recommended, and brought down the house at the wedding.

That, in itself, can be a life-changing experience. When you're "on", and the audience is listening intently, laughing with you and applauding you afterwards, it's incredibly gratifying. And when the bride and groom come up afterwards and tell you how much your tribute meant to them – and how pleased they are that they chose you for the job – the experience takes on an even deeper meaning.

Because in the end, that's what it's all about. Paying tribute to the bride and groom on the biggest day of their lives. It's not about you – it's about them. And you're speaking on behalf of the entire audience in celebrating their marriage and wishing them well.

As I mention throughout this little book, being asked to speak at a wedding is a great honor. Whether you're the best man, the maid of honor or the proud parents of the wedding couple, you can be sure that the bride and groom are counting on you to say something special about them. They also want you to be comfortable in doing so – and classy in your approach.

In the pages that follow, I'm going to help you find the right words; strike the right tone; and discover an inner confidence that you might not even know you possess. The end result is going to be one of the most memorable nights of your life – and a toast that the bride and groom will cherish forever.

VISIT MY WEBSITE FOR MORE TOASTING TIPS

Thank you for purchasing this book – and please note that others in the wedding party can easily purchase the electronic version of *"Wedding Toasts Made Easy"* from my website at **WeddingToasts.com**. The eBook can be downloaded instantly to your computer through a secure, 128-bit encrypted e-commerce system that is used by the world's leading booksellers.

There are many more resources available to you at **WeddingToasts.com** – from a *"Cheat Sheet"* that summarizes all the key points made in this book to a special guided relaxation recording to help you gain confidence in making your toast. Please also note that there's another version of this book geared specifically for those asked to emcee a wedding – it's available at **TheWeddingMCBook.com**.

I wish you the very best of luck at the wedding. Do your homework and make it special for the people getting married. And please let me know how it goes (send an e-mail to me at the address below). Cheers!

Tom Haibeck
tom@haibeck.com

"A toast to the happy couple – and their ability to put that whole ugly 'restraining order' business behind them!"

You've Been Asked to Make a Toast ...

An old friend or relative has just called and asked if you would mind making a toast at an upcoming wedding. Or perhaps you've been asked to serve as Master of Ceremonies at a wedding and have no idea what that involves.

You're honoured to have been asked and have agreed to take on one of those roles. But now, you're starting to panic ...

I've never done this before, you suddenly realize. What's the proper way to make a wedding toast. What does a wedding emcee do? What should I say? Where will I get my material? How long should I speak? What if I bomb in front of my friends and family? What if nobody laughs when I crack a joke?

How will I remember all my lines, let alone everyone's name? What if the microphone doesn't work? Microphone? Yikes, I've never even used a microphone! Why did I ever agree to do this in the first place???

This book has been written to help you through that period of anxiety leading up to the wedding – and to help prepare you to do a first-class job in making that toast and/or in serving as the Master of Ceremonies (or Best Man) at that wedding.

Having spoken at many weddings, dinners and special events, I've developed a pretty good understanding of what works and what doesn't. I've been in your shoes many times and experienced the gut-wrenching anxiety many of you may be feeling in anticipation of the wedding.

I have also enjoyed the honour of being best man at a variety of weddings, so I know what you can expect in that role as well. And finally, I've taken that long trip down the aisle myself, and have vivid memories of how the bride and groom are feeling about now – and what they expect of you.

Reading this book won't turn you into a clone of David Letterman or Conan O'Brien. Nor will it pave the way for you to become a professional emcee or comedian. But it will offer some good, honest, down-to-earth advice on helping the bride and groom make the most of their special day, ensuring the guests enjoy themselves, and preparing you to do the best job you can.

MY PROMISE TO YOU

If you'll take the time to read this book and follow through on the recommended steps and procedures outlined in it, I guarantee you will do an outstanding job with your toast or as Master of Ceremonies. What might feel like an incredible burden to you right now may well turn into one of the greatest nights of your life, for there are few greater joys than to earn the laughter and applause of an appreciative audience.

But more importantly, you will play a pivotal role in the success of the wedding – as through your efforts, the union of those two souls will be celebrated in style at an event that will long be remembered for all the right reasons.

Think of it this way: the bride and groom have entrusted you with a very important responsibility and will expect that you take your job seriously. In helping you through that task, I'm going to ask that you go above and beyond what most people would do. And believe me, it will be worth the effort.

Being asked to speak at a wedding is a great honour. It takes some work, but usually results in a lot of fun, both for you and everyone else involved. Bear that in mind as you read this book and prepare yourself for The Big Day – after all, having fun is what it's all about.

So let's get to lesson one: The Importance of Preparation.

"And Now....
Heeere's Johnny!"

The late Johnny Carson was often referred to as the "King of the Late Night Talk Show Hosts." If you're too young to have seen his show, you can still catch re-runs on many late night cable stations – and believe me, they're well-worth watching.

He was "The Tonight Show" host prior to the guy with the big chin. And for reasons you're about to discover, I think Johnny's show has particular relevance to you right now as you begin preparations to speak at the wedding. Because the secret to Johnny's success as a talk show host is also the secret to your success in making that wedding toast or emceeing the reception.

You see, Johnny made it all *look* so easy. Each night, he would pop out from behind that famous curtain, flash his megawatt grin and ease into his monologue without ever missing a beat. Then it was over to his desk to swap stories with his sidekick, Ed McMahon (who passed away earlier this year). Their conversation never seemed forced – they were just two funny guys who seemed to genuinely like each other.

That kind of easy exchange continued with his guests. His witty repartee with the rich and the famous seemed more like a chat between old friends than a TV interview conducted under hot lights and the pressures of live television.

I loved his show – and carefully studied his technique for my own purposes in going into broadcasting. So when I visited Las Vegas one year and discovered he was the headline act at Caesar's Palace, I HAD to seem him live.

Ironically, I wound up sitting right beside an older fellow who turned out to be one of the senior producers on The Tonight Show. He was incredibly gracious, and seemed to thoroughly enjoy answering the many questions I had about Johnny as we waited for him to take the stage at Caesar's Palace.

THE SECRET TO JOHNNY'S SUCCESS

One of the questions I asked him was "How does he make it all look so easy?" His response: "He works incredibly hard – and does his homework before every show."

My new friend went on to explain that Johnny and his team of writers and producers would spend hours each day talking about the guests that were to appear that night and the topics they would discuss in their interviews.

They would digest detailed summaries of the guest's latest television shows, movies or books; review recent newspaper clippings about them; brainstorm potential gags, one-liners and retorts that might work during the interview; and assemble a list of interview questions that would provide the guest with good conversational material and Johnny with hilarious come-backs.

But they apparently didn't stop there. That kind of studied scripting also extended to Johnny's discussions with co-host, Ed McMahon; his bandleader, Doc Severinsen; and even his executive producer, Fred de Cordova (whom he loved to needle).

MAKING IT LOOK EASY

Certainly much of the material that aired each night was a spontaneous result of Carson's razor-sharp wit. But the fact is, most of the show was planned, scripted and rehearsed each day to make it look unplanned, unscripted and unrehearsed!

And that, ladies and gentlemen, is the secret to making a live performance look easy. You have to do your homework. You have to spend time well in advance of "going live" thinking about what that performance is going to look like. What you're going to say. How you're going to say it. And how your audience is going to react. Then you have to rehearse your material, get comfortable with it and "own" that room when you go live.

I'm telling you this because I'm absolutely convinced that the best wedding speeches (and emcee performances) start and end with that kind of preparation. Our goal is to make it *look* easy – and to offer the kind of thoughtful, polished toast that will honor, inform and entertain your audience with apparent ease. And in order to reach that point, you're going to have to spend some time working on both your material and your delivery.

YOUR WORST NIGHTMARE

Trust me on this: There's nothing worse than being called upon to speak and suddenly realizing that you're completely unprepared (I still have nightmares about that).

Making a wedding toast or speech is very different than simply offering up a spontaneous toast at a family dinner. Because when it's time for you to take the stage and you turn and look back at a ballroom filled with expectant guests, the dynamics are completely different than your family dining room.

There may be 200+ guests peering up at you, in various stages of consciousness; the bride and groom will be on the edge of their seats, praying that you're not going to embarrass them – or yourself; and you will be center stage, the featured speaker at a once-in-a-lifetime event.

If you're not prepared for it, the experience can be truly devestating. Just because you're a naturally funny person who can reel off jokes and recite endless one-liners in the company of your friends does not mean that you will be able to find that same magic in front of a large audience. A trip to your local comedy venue on amateur night can confirm that.

So, be like a Boy Scout – and remember: The secret to success with a wedding toast – the way to make it all *look* easy and natural – is to do your homework and be prepared.

"I've prepared a few notes for my toast ..."

WEDDING TOASTS MADE EASY

The Perfect Wedding Toast

I'm a big believer in the concept of learning by example. If you're trying to learn how to hit a golf ball, for example, it's a good idea to study the pros and get a feel for the mechanics of their swing.

By taking that approach, you will plant a mental image of that perfect swing into your brain – and when it comes time to start learning the mechanics of your own swing, your mind will have a kind of roadmap to follow in moving the club back and swinging through the ball.

The same is true for performing before an audience. If you attend an introductory session of Toastmasters, for example, you will probably spend very little time speaking – but you will have the opportunity to listen to a variety of speeches made by others who have spent more time in the program and refined their speaking abilities.

That exposure will provide a powerful learning experience for you in developing your own speaking style and ability.

Let's apply that to your challenge in making a wedding toast. Many of you reading this book will have attended a wedding at some point that featured an excellent speech or wedding toast.

Think back to that experience for a moment. What moved you about that particular performance? How did the speaker lead you into the toast? What made you laugh – or cry? How was the toast concluded? What do you remember most about it? And what made it so effective?

You needn't try to duplicate that exact toast – you're going to develop your own material. But the style and content of that toast may well give you some excellent food-for-thought (and mental imagery) to draw upon in preparing your own toast.

Let me give you an example. One of the best wedding speeches I've ever witnessed was at the wedding of my brother-in-law. His best man delivered a toast that quite literally had the audience in hysterics with his rollicking account of *"Growing Up with the Groom."*

He told us of their mischievous childhood pranks, their outrageous competition for girlfriends, their ineptitude in waiting tables together in a restaurant, and their buffoonery in sinking a sailboat (they apparently forgot about the tide one night when they dropped anchor next to a rocky shoreline).

He concluded with a few earnest thoughts about what their life-long friendship had meant to him, and offered that if the prevailing force in any good marriage is a solid friendship between husband and wife – then theirs would last a lifetime, for John (the groom) had indeed proven to be an exceptional friend. It was simple, enlightening, humorous and consistent. And the audience loved it!

SAY IT FROM THE HEART

Another key element of that speech was the fact that it was made from the heart – and based upon some very real human experience. That's often a better choice than trying to be funny (if you're not a naturally funny person).

That bit of advice was beautifully illustrated in one of the seminal scenes from the movie *"Wedding Crashers."* The maid of honor decides she's going to take a humorous approach in making her toast to the bride (her sister). Owen Wilson, who plays the suave rogue who crashes weddings in search of desperate, single women, hears some of her material (while she's rehearsing it) and quickly senses it's not funny. "Honestly, I think you're better off going for something from the heart," he warns her. "I think people are going to love this," she replies.

WEDDING TOASTS MADE EASY

They don't – and she's a disaster. Her jokes fall flat and the guests grow hostile with her attemtps at sarcasm. Finally, she relents and takes Wilson's advice. Slowly, she wins over the audience by simply telling them how much she loves her sister, and how happy she is for her in finding the right guy to marry.

Sincerity works. And so does simplicity. But if humor is your chosen genre, then I would strongly recommend that you use anecdotal stories rather than canned jokes.

"THIS ONE TIME, AT BAND CAMP ..."

In fact, I believe anecdotal material is the best source of humor for a wedding toast or speech. Any speaker becomes far more eloquent with the retelling of a story that he or she has personally experienced. And the audience at a wedding reception loves to hear those kind of real-life stories (providing they are in reasonably good taste).

You were there – you saw him or her sink the sailboat or drop the hot bowl of soup on the customer's lap – and as a result, you will tell those stories in your own words, and in a far more real and compelling manner than you would in telling a joke (that's because a joke typically involves the retelling of a made-up story that has no real connection to you; most jokes also rely on superb timing to make the punch line work, and most people have difficulty with that before a large audience).

I've also noticed over the years that most people tend to automatically become more animated and amused in the re-telling of their own stories. They begin to smile and laugh as the memories emerge, and the audience tends to laugh along with them. The lampooned groom starts to blush and squirm; his new bride shrieks with every new twist to the outrageous tale; his family and friends are hysterical with the shared memory of it all; and the new in-laws start to feel better about the guy marrying into their family, knowing he's a bit of a doofus.

But remember: Humor doesn't HAVE to be a part of any wedding toast or speech; if you're not a particularly funny person, go with the more earnest approach.

"And isn't that a beautiful bride's dress? Must have
cost a fortune — all that extra material."

WEDDING TOASTS MADE EASY

Toasting 101: The Basics

As you might have noticed by now, I've included some cartoons in this book to help illustrate how NOT to make a wedding toast. Just think of him as Uncle Buck, the slightly inebriated uncle of the bride who says and does all the wrong things.

If you remember one thing from this book, make it this: Our purpose in offering a wedding toast is to honor the person (or persons) to whom it is offered. We want to leave them feeling good about themselves – rather than hurt or humiliated.

That doesn't mean you can't have some fun with your toast – or gently tease or poke a little fun at someone – but the ultimate purpose of a wedding toast is to honor the bride and groom and to help celebrate their marriage.

This isn't a roast for the groom. Nor is it an excuse to get back at your older sister by recounting her previous dating adventures. And it's most certainly not a platform for you to try to launch your career as a comedian. This is about the bride and groom, and the bringing together of their family and friends on the most important day of their lives. So please remember that this is the wedding part – not the bachelors at the bar part.

Also remember to keep your toast short and simple – and to be yourself. Far too many people strive to become someone they're not in making a toast. Quoting flowery passages from famous speeches, they try to emulate the oratory excellence of a Lincoln or a Churchill but end up sounding like a pompous fool.

It's far better, in my opinion, to use your own words in expressing your thoughts. Those canned toasts that you can buy on the Internet can never replace the kind of warmth, intimacy and authenticity of a toast that you craft on your own. Besides that, 99% of the people who try to use a canned wedding speech are going to sound canned and insincere when they deliver it.

Think about it: You have a wealth of material to work with in preparing your toast. As the individual chosen for the task, you are probably very familiar with the background and character of the bride, or the groom, or whomever you are toasting; use that anecdotal information to make a warm, personalized toast.

"THEN THERE WAS THE TIME ..."

At our wedding, the person who made the toast to the bride was a close friend of my wife's family. He told a few humorous stories about her when she was a little girl and then related how he had watched her grow up to become the mature, sophisticated woman she is today. It was a very moving toast, made simply and from the heart.

That's the kind of speech audiences love to hear at a wedding reception. It's an emotional day for all concerned, and people have a right to be sentimental as they celebrate the day. But bear in mind that balance is also important – in the same way that some people sometimes go too far in trying to be funny, other people can get carried away with the schmaltzy stuff.

THE SATURDAY NIGHT SERMON

Ditto for religious diatribes – I once attended a wedding at which the father of the groom decided to deliver a discourse on spirituality (as part of his wedding toast) that ran over twenty minutes long. A short prayer or recital of a brief religious passage may be appropriate, but save us all from the Saturday night sermons.

While on that subject, I want to clarify what I said earlier on the concept of using famous quotations. A good quote can be an effective platform upon which to build a speech. But again, just don't overdo it. I've heard people try to weave together a dozen or more of these lofty pronouncements, and the result is usually the same. They sound phoney and over-the-top.

END ON A POSITIVE NOTE

If you decide on the humorous approach, remember to conclude your toast on a more serious, upbeat note that honors the recipient. For example, if the balance of your speech recounts a series of humorous traits or misadventures of the groom, be sure to end it with some sincere praise for him.

Talk about why you admire him, what his friendship has meant to you, why he will make an excellent partner for his new bride and how much you'll miss him now that he's married (remember to duck if you use that one).

It's also a good idea to poke a little fun at yourself before teasing someone else. If you're polite, gracious and somewhat self-deprecating in your remarks (and thus willing to demonstrate that you are capable of laughing at some of your own particular foibles), the audience will be far more willing to laugh along with you should you lob a few gentle jibes at someone else.

TIME YOURSELF

A wedding speech need never be longer than five minutes, in my opinion. Unless the speaker is exceptionally good, the audience will quickly lose interest beyond that point. As a general rule of thumb, I would encourage people to try to make their toast between three to five minutes (or less). Time yourself while rehearsing your speech to develop a feel for its length.

When making your toast, maintain eye contact with your audience and look around the room so everyone feels included. Also be sure to occasionally look at the person to whom you're giving the toast to help focus attention on that individual (or the wedding couple). That will honor the recipient(s), and take some of the pressure off of you while making the toast.

"TO THE BRIDE & GROOM!"

Some people make brilliant speeches leading up to their toast and then seem unsure what to say in proposing the actual toast. Remember that the conclusion of a toast is like a call to action; you must give the audience some direction. After delivering your speech, ask the guests to rise (if they are seated). Give them plenty of time to do so. Then focus your attention on the subject of your toast, raise your glass and ask the audience to join with you in toasting the new bride/the new couple/the bridesmaids or whomever. *"Ladies and gentlemen, please join me in a toast to the bride"* or *"Ladies and gentlemen, to the bride and groom!"* Take a small sip of your beverage, smile back at your subject(s) and quietly return to your seat.

BE KIND TO AUNT EDNA

A word of advice on the standing-up part: If there are to be multiple toasts at the wedding reception, and people are seated, you should probably avoid asking guests to rise for each toast.

That process will get tiresome – and for elderly people (or those who have joined Uncle Buck at the open bar), it can be difficult to repeatedly rise from their table and stand to participate in a toast. If that is the case, simply conclude your toast with a brief pause (count one, two, three), turn and smile at the recipient of the toast, and say: *"Please join me ... in raising your glasses ... as we salute the marriage of Bob & Carol!"* (or some version of that).

And dumb as it sounds, remember to bring your glass with you if you are called to the podium to make a toast. It's downright embarrassing to make your brilliant speech and then suddenly realize you have no glass to raise in concluding your toast (somehow an "air toast" just doesn't have the same effect). Use a wine glass or champagne flute, even if you're drinking juice or soda. A classy toast deserves to be made with an elegant glass.

LET'S HOPE THEY GET IT RIGHT THIS TIME

Some other dumb mistakes to avoid: If it's the bride and/or groom's second marriage, don't mention their first marriage. Believe it or not, people can be a little sensitive about their first failed attempt at marital bliss. If it's their third or fourth, however, they may have developed a sense of humor about it all by then (but check with them first).

Don't get into any embarrassing speculation about their honeymoon or the recreational opportunities they might pursue behind closed doors. Avoid any references to the bride's weight, shoe size, past boyfriends or her recent appearance on the Jerry Springer Show. And remember that it's exceptionally bad etiquette to try to toast and chew gum at the same time (ditch the gum).

THE ORDER OF WEDDING TOASTS

I have included a separate chapter on how to plan a wedding reception for best results. But here's a synopsis of who makes toasts, and the order in which they are made.

The bride's father might open by thanking guests for attending, welcoming his new son into the family and proposing a toast to his daughter. The best man might then offer a tribute to the new couple. The maid of honor could follow with her own tribute to them. Then the groom might respond, as may the bride (or the bride and groom could speak as a couple).

Bear in mind, though, that there is no legal requirement or societal bylaw that demands such an order of toasts. Do what works for you and your family – it's your wedding, and it needn't be complicated by an obsession with etiquette. If you prefer a more relaxed, spontaneous approach, go for it!

SPONTANEOUS TOASTS

Other friends and family members may also want to speak – but I'd suggest that the couple try to limit the number of toasts, as too many can get tiresome. If it's a large wedding (over 50 people), I would also strongly recommend that an event agenda be prepared to identify both the timing for the toasts and the specific individuals that have been pre-approved to offer a toast. That way, the emcee can control access to the microphone.

THE OPEN MICROPHONE

At some weddings, the pre-arranged series of toasts are followed by an "open microhone" session at which anyone present is invited to offer a toast or tell a favorite story about the bride and groom. That can be a lot fun – but take a careful read on your audience before going there. If it's a rowdy bunch and the reception features an open bar, an open microphone can be an open invitation to disaster.

A final note: The people being toasted do not participate in the actual toast. They do not stand or raise their glasses or sip their drink – they should simply smile and nod back at the audience with a gracious *"Thank You!"*

"Hey you two! Give us a little preview of what's gonna happen later tonight in the old bridal suite!"

Types of
Wedding Toasts

At some weddings, there may only be one single toast – and that would be to the new couple. But at most weddings, there are a variety of different toasts made to a variety of special individuals.

If you're reading this book, you've probably been asked to make one of those toasts. It could be the toast to the bride; or a toast to the groom; a toast to the bridesmaids; or a toast from you, the father of the bride. So in the pages ahead, I'm going to discuss each of those particular toasts (and a few others) to examine some of the key features and subtle nuances of each one.

If you wish, simply skip over to the material in this chapter that deals with the particular toast you have been chosen to give. In the interests of being better prepared, however, it would probably be a good idea to read through the entire chapter in order to develop a better understanding of what others might be saying in their particular toasts.

You see, each of the different "participants" in the wedding has a different role to play in the event – and a different set of expectations about both the day itself and their part in it. And as a consequence, the subject matter for the toast to the bride will probably be considerably different than the words chosen to thank the bridesmaids.

But the one constant in each of those toasts is this: Every one of those participants wants to feel acknowledged and honoured as part of the tribute made to them on The Big Day. Bear that in mind as you think about the toast you're about to make.

PRETEND IT'S YOUR OWN WEDDING

Before we get into a discussion about the various kinds of wedding toasts, step back for a moment and pretend this is your own wedding. What would you want people to say about you?

Would you would want your friends and family members to say some nice things about you and to congratulate you on finding such an ideal mate? Would you would want to feel welcomed and accepted into your new family? Would you secretly wish that your brother or best friend might razz you a bit about your eccentricities or misadventures? And would you want your guests to laugh, be entertained, and made to feel part of the shared joy of your wedding?

Of course you would. So try to build some or all of those elements into your toast. Here are some thoughts on each one of the various "wedding genre" toasts. And brides, please don't feel that you have to include all of these at your wedding; if you do, try to keep the total time allocated to toasts and speeches to a maximum of about twenty minutes (or less). Also make sure to prepare an agenda (more on that later).

THE TOAST TO THE BRIDE

This is, without question, the most important toast of the day. She is The Princess – and this is the day she has dreamed about since she was a little girl. Help make her day even more special by doing her proud with your toast.

If you have been given the honor of making this toast, consider it an incredible honor and privilege. You have no doubt been chosen for the job because you know her well, and have been an important part of her life.

You might be the bride's father, a favorite uncle, a close friend of the family or the bride's roommate from college. And during the course of your toast, she is counting on you to celebrate her as an individual; to share some observations about her life and your history with her; and to author a kind of collective Hallmark card from everyone in attendance to say how wonderful she looks and how happy everyone is for her.

This is a toast that can often be a bit emotional – for the person offering it, the bride herself and the guests in attendance. After all, it's not the blushing groom that brings the tears; it's the beautiful bride in the flowing white gown, the little girl who has become a woman. If you – or the audience or the bride herself – get a little teary, go with it.

Be gentle with the bride. I would avoid teasing her too much or saying anything that could offend her (unless she, herself, has a great sense of humor and the two of you have a history of kidding each other). Congratulate her on finding such a great guy to marry; tell her new husband how lucky he is to have married her; flatter her and tell her how gorgeous she looks; and wish the new couple well as they start their new life together.

THE BEST MAN'S SPEECH

As mentioned, the Toast to the Bride is the most important toast of the day. But the best man is typically the featured speaker.

Again, if you have been asked to serve as the best man, consider it a great honor. That's probably a good starting point for your speech, as well (after you have introduced yourself and told the audience your relationship to the groom – friend, brother, fellow airline passenger). Tell the groom how honored you are to have been asked to be his best man (look him square in the eye when you tell him so – even if you did just meet him on the plane).

You might also thank the bride's parents for their efforts in arranging such a splendid event; and if you have grown up with the groom and are close to his parents, thank them, as well, for the rehearsal dinner (and for the hospitality they offered to you while growing up with their son). You should also express your admiration for the bride, and tell the groom how she completes him and is so good for him (say it with a straight face).

But the primary target ... er, focus of your speech is, of course, the groom. The audience wants to get a sense of the bonding and brotherhood between the two of you. They want to know something of your history as friends, perhaps how the two of you met and some of the goofy things you did together.

"THEN WE MET THESE BABES ..."

They want to laugh and be entertained by your speech – but only within the confines of good taste (humiliating stories from the bachelor's dinner, ribald tales from the roadtrips you took together and any mention of previous girlfriends are strictly off-limits. Ditto for any mention of ex-wives, excess flatulence or advice on consummating the marriage). Remember, this isn't a roast for the groom. It's a tribute to him on his wedding day.

Some final notes on the best man's speech: If you're not naturally funny, don't feel like you have to be. And if you're not particularly comfortable speaking to an audience, just keep your toast short and sweet (you can say a lot in thirty seconds). Also, it might be a good idea to ask the bride and groom to stand next to you while toasting them (providing your toast isn't overly long).

THE GROOM'S RESPONSE

While it might be tempting to try to ad lib and match wits with the best man's quips about you, my advice is to stick with the script (which you will have prepared well in advance of the wedding). Unless you're a particulary accomplished speaker who can develop and deliver funny responses on the fly, never try to wing it on your wedding day.

Now that doesn't mean you can't anticipate some of the best man's barbs and have a few pre-written (and well-rehearsed) shots of your own (I'm assuming the two of you are willing to stoop to this level). The audience is going to expect a little good-natured banter between the two of you, so feel free to have some fun with your speech (but say some nice things, as well).

The most important elements of your speech are to thank: the best man, the bridesmaids and other members of the wedding party for "being there" for you and your wife; your new in-laws for welcoming you into their family and for hosting the wedding; your own parents for all they've done for you; and your new wife for agreeing to marry you (don't forget to gush a little and to tell her your knees buckled when you turned and saw her walking down the aisle). One thing: Do not cry. Under any circumstances. It's against the code. See Rule 38.

THE MAID OF HONOUR'S SPEECH

One of the things I've noticed recently is that more and more women are being asked to speak at weddings. That's decidedly different than a decade ago. I think it has a lot to do with the fact that so many more women have advanced in their careers and have become good at making presentations; therefore, it's often a natural extension for them to speak at a wedding.

Like the best man, your subject matter is probably going to be about your relationship with the bride. No doubt the stories you might tell about your history together would be a little different than the ones offered by the best man (although I've heard some rather raunchy tales of late from "the girls" and their exploits). Have fun; but keep it within the bounds of good taste.

Also, don't forget to acknowledge the other bridesmaids and to tell the bride how stunning she looks (even if she just looks stunned). You might also want to offer some positive comments about the groom and mention his good fortune in marrying the bride. Wish them well, then raise your glass to them.

THE BRIDE'S RESPONSE

This is strictly optional. The bride is under no obligation to make a toast or speech at her own wedding. But if you choose to say a few words, see above ("The Groom's Response").

It's best to prepare your remarks in advance, to keep them fairly short and sweet, and to be gracious and thank others (especially the guests for taking the time to attend the wedding, for their good wishes and for the gifts they have lavished upon you).

It's also a good idea to tell your new husband how much you love him (even if he did chose to go with the white shoe option on the tux rental) and to perhaps declare, before your family and friends, your enduring love for him. You will also win a year's worth of brownie points by saluting your new in-laws.

Option: The bride and groom might do their speech together, thanking others and then taking turns to pay a brief tribute to each other. Finish by interlocking your arms for a toast (or not).

THE FATHER OF THE BRIDE THANKS GUESTS

This is no doubt an emotional day for you, Pop. You've given away your little girl – that sweet little bundle of joy who was just entering Grade One a couple of weeks ago. Where did the time go? And who is this yutz she's just married?

I was once asked on an open-line radio show what the father of the bride should do if he feels himself getting teary while delivering his speech. In one of those *"I wish I'd said this"* moments on the way home, I thought to myself: "The best way for you (the father of the bride) to avoid tears is to bring a copy of the bill (for the reception) along with you to the podium. As soon as you start getting choked up, have a peek at the bill – that will tend to drain the sentiment right out of you."

What I actually said on the show – and what I continue to believe today – is that it's perfectly acceptable for the father of the bride to get a little emotional when speaking at his daughter's wedding (no code violation there, Dad).

If you need a moment, simply pause, take a sip of water, gaze over at that beautiful daughter of yours and focus on being thankful for her health and the opportunity to have raised her. Have a look at her new husband, as well; the thought of him joining you for Sunday night dinner the rest of your life might also provide the sobering effect you'll need at that point.

Seriously, though, the main focus of your toast is to be the class act that thanks guests for attending, pays tribute to your daughter and welcomes your new son-in-law into the family (try to say something nice about him, now that you've put away the shotgun).

Also offer some welcoming words to the groom's family; thank guests for attending the wedding; thank the various people that have helped plan and organize the wedding; and perhaps offer a few thoughts on the meaning of marriage and/or a couple of funny stories about the joys of raising your daughter. Then tell everyone how proud you are of her and wish her the very best with the yutz ... I mean splendid fellow ... that she married.

TOASTS FROM OTHER FAMILY MEMBERS

The mothers of the new couple might also want to wish them well – as might other friends and family members. But as you have probably gathered by now, there are potentially a lot of people who might want to speak at the wedding, and frankly, that can get tiresome. One way to prevent that is to prepare an agenda and instruct the emcee or disc jockey not to give the microphone to anyone not listed on the agenda.

TOASTS AT THE REHEARSAL DINNER

Another effective way to cut down on the time allocated to wedding toasts is to schedule some of them for the rehearsal dinner (rather than the wedding reception). That could be a better option, in many cases, as the rehearsal dinner is typically more informal (with a lot fewer activities to try to include). It's also a good time to try to create some bonding between the two families, and toasts can be a great tool for that.

BRIEF YOUR TOASTERS

Brides, take note: Brief all of your wedding day toasters with an e-mail four to six weeks in advance of the wedding. Thank them for agreeing to speak at the wedding, then give them some orientation and set some parameters by including an agenda, along with the following information:

- Date/time/location of reception (with map, if needed)
- Description of event venue (ballroom? patio? restaurant?)
- Whether a sound-system will be available
- Whether a lectern or podium will be available
- If no podium, where they should stand when toasting
- If they can rehearse in the venue prior to the reception
- Whether someone will introduce them prior to their toast
- Number of guests expected; brief description of audience
- Note any concerns about offending elderly guests
- Number of toasts to be made (and to whom)
- Suggested length of toasts
- Contact information as needed

You might also want to suggest they purchase their own copy of this book. They can instantly download the eBook at WeddingToasts.com.

"Hey everybody! The cake's cut.
Now it's time for the food fight!"

Themes for a Wedding Toast

Remember how your Grade Ten teacher harped at you about the need to develop a specific theme for your essay? Well, guess what: The same principle applies to writing an effective speech.

Good speechwriters know that an audience can only grasp a limited amount of information at any one sitting – and that one of the best ways to grab and hold their attention is by throwing out a theme statement and structuring their speech around that.

I encourage you to consider the same principle in preparing your wedding toast or speech. Pick a theme – and build your talk around that particular theme (I'm going to suggest some appropriate wedding-related themes to use later in this chapter; *"How to Win Friends & Marry for Money"* isn't one of them).

To help get you started, log onto HistoryChannel.com. Sponsored by the television program, *"The History Channel"*, this website offers commentary, text and actual recreations of some of history's greatest speeches:

- **Winston Churchill** rallying a nation around a theme of *"We Shall Never Surrender"*

- **Martin Luther King** inspiring social reform with his famous speech *"I Have a Dream"*

- **President John F. Kennedy's** stirring inaugural speech with his famous appeal: *"Ask not what your country can do for you — ask what you can do for your country!"*

Now certainly no wedding speech or toast need be as serious or dramatic as any of those examples. But in the same way that those speeches were written around a central theme – and given life through the insertion of brilliant analogies, colorful metaphors and the use of short, crisp sentences – so too can your wedding speech benefit from those same time-honored principles.

ATTENTION DEFICIT THROUGH DRINKING DISORDER

Communicating with an audience at a wedding reception has particular challenges. Many guests may be experiencing the infamous *"attention-deficit-through-drinking-disorder-syndrome"* – resulting in a certain degree of difficulty in following the spoken word. (The good news is that they may be more inclined to find humor in your lame jokes and droll one-liners). Make it easy for them to tune into your toast by working with a theme.

The other major reason why it makes sense to build your toast around a theme is that it helps you to stay focused in writing and delivering it.

FINDING A FOCUS FOR YOUR SPEECH

By choosing a theme, you will immediately begin to hone in on what you want to say. You will have a consistent body of thought from which to draw your inspirations and organize your key points.

And when it comes time to deliver your toast, you will do so with greater confidence, knowing that your speech is going to follow a clear-cut, well-defined path of information that will be easy for your audience to follow (they don't have the benefit of being able to rewind and re-listen to your speech).

Remember the all-time best wedding speech I referenced earlier? It had a theme – and was built around the best man's wry recollections of *"Growing Up with the Groom."* That's a theme that I've used as well – and one that might also work for you in developing a theme for your own speech.

Take a moment right now and start to think about your toast. Is there any particular theme that you might use to build your speech around? Any colorful memories or stories that jump out at you? Any tendencies or behavourial patterns that emerge about your subject?

WEDDING TOASTS MADE EASY

If not, here are nine proven themes for you to consider in building your wedding toast or speech:

- **Friendship** – What do you remember most about your experience with the bride, the groom or the person being honored? What happened that was funny? What did you learn from your friendship? What makes this person such a good friend? How will that demonstrated history of friendship translate into a promising marriage?

- **How They Met** – People at a wedding reception love to hear stories about how the couple met, their courtship, how and where The Big Question was popped, wedding jitters, etc. You might want to twist the facts a bit for comedic relief ("You perhaps weren't aware that Bob met Carol in a knitting class he'd signed-up for.")

- **Watching Them Grow** – For an older person who has personally witnessed the growth of a younger person (uncle; aunt; grandparent; neighbor; minister; parole officer), there may be a wealth of fascinating material to share, such as their birth, early childhood, education, first jobs, old flames, new hairpiece. Remember to also make mention of how the couple has grown since they met.

- **Prescription for a Successful Marriage** – We can all benefit from words of wisdom about what it takes to build and sustain a happy marriage. You might tackle this on the basis of your own experience or through researching the subject matter with someone you know that has a long and particularly successful marriage.

- **Why They're Good for Each Other** – The individuals in a marriage tend to complement one another. And in many cases, it's fair to say they actually complete each other. Opposites do attract, and the strengths in one partner may well be the weaknesses in the other. That kind of phenomena offers some excellent material or your toast, as it provides the opportunity to make both some positive observations about the bride and groom and to take a more humorous approach in exploring some of their quirks and eccentricities.

- **A Toast to Love & Laughter & Happily Ever-After** – If you wish to keep your toast short and sweet, you might simply offer your sincere wishes for the new couple to live a life together based on the above. That's also a great theme to use in discussing the new couple's relationship and in wishing them a happy future together.

- **Famous Quotations** – These are my least favorite option for thematic material because they lack the personalized and more experiential qualities of those described above. But if you're not comfortable making a speech or telling a story, recounting the wise words of others *can* prove both informative and entertaining for your audience. Here's a few samples; there are many more in the back of the book.

"May you grow old together on one pillow."
– Armenian Proverb

"Never above you. Never below you. Always beside you."
– Walter Winchell

"The greatest of all arts is the art of living together."
– William Lyon Phelps

A final thought on content for your speech or toast: As any good presenter knows, visuals can be a highly effective means to reinforce key points and keep your audience involved. Why not apply the same techniques to your presentation at the wedding?

By using a software program such as PowerPoint (you're welcome, Mr. Gates), you can put together a series of pictures and text to tell the life story of the person(s) you are honoring (another option is to use old video from their childhood). Start with those embarrassing baby pictures and then progress through the rest of their life, using the occasional text slide to transition into new eras or to inject humorous asides.

For some truly brilliant examples of transition slides, have a look at some old re-runs of the *"Frasier"* show; the creative team used clever headlines to introduce each new scene, and the effect was often hilarious. The design of those screen transitions was also very effective (reverse white type on a black screen).

A SAMPLE SPEECH BY THE BEST MAN

Here's the full text version of a tribute I once gave when asked to serve as the best man. The point-form version follows – and that's the one I would have used at the reception itself. I have written this one out word-for-word in order to give you a better feel for its content and how it would sound when delivered.

The theme for the speech is friendship. It's similar to the one I've just described in the previous chapter – and again, the audience loved it. They learned some things about the groom that they hadn't known before – as mentioned, wedding guests tend to enjoy learning more about the people involved in the event.

Note the short, crisp sentences. That makes them a lot easier to deliver. Also note the areas where I would pause – I try to count to three (in my head) after I've delivered a funny line or when I'm attempting to emphasize a key point.

Please also note the fact that I have interspersed some positive observations about the groom amongst my many gentle barbs about our history. In our case, we have always enjoyed a lot of kibitzing back and forth, so it was certainly fitting for me to prod him a little at his wedding. But I also wanted to recognize some of his positive attributes and accomplishments (despite how difficult they were to identify). The speech concludes with a few heartfelt thoughts about our life-long friendship.

A Toast to the Groom

Harry and I met while we were in kindergarten. He was the skinny kid with the glasses and big feet.

I remember him well. When our kindergarten teacher asked us what we wanted to be when we grew up, most of us said we wanted to become a fireman or a cowboy or an astronaut.

But not Harry. He puffed up his chest and proclaimed: "I want to be an Attorney at Law, practicing civil litigation."

I swear he said that. He really did. He just seemed so ... precocious.

For example, while we were learning the alphabet, he was studying class action suits and the law of torts.

Harry's mastery of the law came in handy a few years later when he filed a claim against our Grade Three teacher for unlawful confinement. She laughed so hard she actually let us out a few minutes early from the detention she had given us.

His childhood hero was Howard Cosell. I'm serious. Howard Cosell! Harry liked the fact that he knew so much about sports ... that he was argumentative ... and that he was a lawyer!

It's said that our childhood heroes often have a bearing on who we become as adults. In Harry's case, that's certainly true. Like his hero, Howard, he's insufferable with his knowledge of sports. Totally argumentative. And of course, he's a lawyer.

By the way, does anyone know how to save a drowning lawyer? (pause). Good!

Anyway, as I mentioned, Harry always seemed to know what he wanted. He was our Class Valedictorian in Grade Nine. He made the football team ... and the basketball team ... despite his hopelessly limited athletic ability.

High school was another matter. As always, Harry excelled in school. And he continued to make the most of his meager athletic abilities.

But something very fundamental about him changed in Grade Ten. Something that took us all by surprise ... and changed his life ... forever.

Harry discovered the magic of ... contact lenses! Yes, our former four-eyed friend lost his Coke bottle glasses and nerdy demeanor. It was kind of like Clark Kent going into the phone booth. He became someone totally new.

In Harry"s case, that new persona was ... well, I was going to say "chick magnet" but that would be stretching it. Let"s just say he suddenly hit the radar screens of a few desperate schoolgirls.

He also managed to hit a lot of walls. Literally! His transition from Coke bottle glasses to Coke bottle lenses wasn't without its challenges for Harold, and he managed to run smack into his share of walls that year.

And we'll never forget the day he mistakenly made his way into the Girl's locker room. Or at least, he claimed it was a mistake!

Harry managed to hit his share of books as well, and he graduated from high school with first-class honors.

College was next. He earned a Degree in Business ... along with several scholarships. He also earned the title of *"Designated Drinker"* in his particular fraternity (Phi Beta Budweiser).

To cap his academic achievements, Harry was accepted into one the top law schools in this country. He was apparently the only applicant in the history of that school to submit a resume starting from the time he was in kindergarten ... and included the decision by our Grade Three teacher to reduce our sentence.

As we all know, Harold met his future bride-to-be at law school. And over the next three years, he discovered a part of life that proved to be even more interesting than the law. He found love.

He and Carol became insufferable ... I mean, inseparable. They sat together. Studied together. Ate together. And began to wear matching hot pink outfits together. They were truly adorable.

And they look adorable here, today ... even if they're not still wearing hot pink. But in all seriousness, Harry is one of my oldest and best friends. He's like a brother to me ... and we've been through a lot together.

Through those years, he's always been there for me. And I know he will always be there for Carol.

Ladies & gentlemen, I would like to invite you to rise ... and to join with me ... in offering a toast ... to our dear friend, Harry ... and his beautiful new bride. To Harry and Carol!

The following page offers a point-form version of that same speech. Note how I've used single words or phrases to trigger my thoughts. That enables me to to deliver it in a much more natural style than reading it word-for-word from a prepared text. Try it – you'll find it enables you to tell those stories rather than reading them.

TOAST TO THE GROOM

- Kindergarten. Glasses. Big Feet.
- Fireman. Cowboy. Astronaut.
- Attorney at Law/Civil Litigation.

- Swear he said that. Precocious. History of Torts.
- Unlawful confinement. Sprung us loose from detention.

- Hero – Howard Cosell.
- Sports. Argue. Lawyer.
- Childhood heroes. Insufferable. Argumentative. Lawyer.
- Drowning lawyer? Good!

- Valedictorian.
- Made football/basketball teams – despite limited athletic ability.

- High school. Excelled.
- Made most of meager athletic ability.
- Fundamental change. Took us all by surprise.
- Discovered magic of – contact lenses!

- Former four-eyed friend.
- Lost Coke bottle lenses/nerdy demeanor.
- Clark Kent going into phone booth.
- Chick magnet. Hit radar screens of desperate schoolgirls. Also walls.

- Also hit books – honors.
- Commerce Degree. Designated drinker.

- Top law school. Resume from kindergarten. Reduce our sentence.
- Met Bride-to-be. Carol.

- Found something even more interesting than the law. Love.
- He & Carol became insufferable/inseparable.
- Sat together. Studied. Ate. Hot pink. Adorable.

- Adorable today. No hot pink.
- One of oldest & best friends. Brother.
- Been through a lot together.

- Always been there. Will be for Carol.
- Toast to the Groom/beautiful new Bride.
- To Harry & Carol!

Writing Your Wedding Toast

So now that we've covered the basics about wedding toasts and taken a look at some examples of other successful toasts, it's time to put pen to paper for yours.

I'm hoping that you're reading this well in advance of the wedding so that you have plenty of time to pull your thoughts together. As those thoughts come to mind, be sure to write them down. Those memories and ideas that pop into your head for speech material may drift away if you don't record them.

I like to carry a specific notebook for this purpose; another option is to set up a file to store your notes or to perhaps carry a portable dictaphone with you. Please take action on one of those options – you'll kick yourself for not doing so when it comes time to try to recall those hilarious stories and observations.

After you've spent a few weeks thinking about your presentation, you'll probably have several pages of notes to sift through and organize. Plan to spend a few hours in a quiet place with a pen and a notepad and your file of collected thoughts.

Read through those notes and try to identify four or five good anecdotes; also take a read through the final chapter of this book, which contains hundreds of suggested one-liners, quotes and famous sayings about marriage.

Try to avoid the temptation to write your speech word-for-word. Instead, put together a point-form outline for your toast, like the sample one on the opposite page. Unless you plan to speak for a considerable time, limit your outline to a single page.

Toast or tribute? First of all, let's differentiate between a wedding toast and a tribute. A wedding toast can be as simple as *"To the bride and groom: May your love last forever!"* A tribute, on the other hand, offers a bit more. We pay tribute to the person(s) we are honoring by making a little speech, which is concluded with a toast.

Keep it short. As previously mentioned, a tribute need never go longer than five minutes (unless the speaker is *exceptionally* good). Three to four minutes is about right for most people – but you can say a lot in as little as sixty seconds. Talk to the bridal couple about how long they expect you to speak.

Consider the environment. If the reception is to feature a formal sit-down dinner, then a longer tribute is probably going to be acceptable. But if it's an informal gathering at an outdoor location with questionable accoustics, plan to keep it short.

Consider your audience. Good speakers always take the time to do some research on their audience. Find out how many people will be attending the wedding. And in general terms, try to determine: Where are they from? How old are they? What do they do for a living? Are they fun-loving or conservative? High society or just regular folks? Elderly and/or easily offended?

Use index cards to organize your notes. They're much easier to handle and organize. Use a pencil, to allow for last-minute changes or deletions. Number the cards so that you can quickly put them back in order should you arrive at the podium and drop them. Also place a heading on each card for easy reference (e.g. "Kindergarten Story" or "Harry Gets Contact Lenses").

Make it flow. Try to lead your audience through your tribute in a way that makes it easy for them to follow and understand what you're saying. Use transitions from one section to the next. For example, if your theme is friendship and you're discussing the nature of your own friendship with the groom, connect that with his worthiness as a husband and best friend to his new wife (*"Through those years, he's always been there for me. And I know he will always be there for Carol"*).

Listen as you write. Good speechwriters read their speech aloud as they write it. Is it warm and conversational, or stiff and pompous? Are your sentences short and punchy, or long and cumbersome? Is there a nice flow to your delivery, or does it sound choppy and disorganized? Keep it simple. And avoid using big words (obfuscate) when simple ones (confuse) will do.

Structure your tribute. A good speech has a beginning, a middle and an end. We want to have an opening that will grab the audience's attention, some shared stories or insights that will carry the balance of your tribute, and a closing section to wish the couple well. I'll discuss each of those in more detail as we progress through this section.

Introduce yourself. Find out if there will be an emcee at the wedding that will introduce you prior to your toast. If not, plan to introduce yourself, mentioning your name, your relationship to the bride and groom (brother, uncle, friend, co-worker, cell mate) and perhaps what you do and where you live. Guests want to know that information so they can "place" you and get a sense of context for your remarks.

It's about them. Always remember that the wedding and reception are in honor of the bride and groom. They're the stars, not you. While it certainly makes sense to introduce yourself and to discuss your relationship with the couple, don't make the mistake of droning on and on about yourself.

Develop a punchy opening. After your introduction, plan to open with something punchy that will engage the audience. A quick little anecdote, a good one-liner or a thoughtful quote or observation about the couple, or the wedding, or the venue.

Use one-liners. Witty one-liners are much easier to work with than canned jokes. And that's especially true at the start of your toast; if you mess up that long, complicated yarn and nobody gets the punchline, you're going to be off to a horrible start. I've included a whole treasury of suggested wedding-related quotes and one-liners at the back of the book. Take a read through them and highlight the ones that you think you might use.

Share some funny stories. Connect your opening to the rest of the toast with a few funny stories, observations or words of advice for the bride or groom (*"As some of you know, the groom tends to snore in his sleep. I know this because I slept in the room next to him for 18 years. So being that my new sister-in-law is about to discover that phenomena, I thought I'd describe some of the coping mechanisms I've developed over the years to drown out my brother, Brad, the human buzz saw ..."*). Human interest stories sell newspapers; it also makes for great wedding tributes.

Use appropriate humor. If you plan to go for some laughs, remember to keep it in good taste. The jokes you told at the groom's stag probably won't go over well with the bride's grandmother. If the content of a joke or story could prove offensive to even one person in that audience, my advice is not to use it. Also remember to watch the actual language that you use in telling jokes or stories (no swearing; no jargon). And be careful not to resort to a lot of "inside" humor that only a few people will understand and appreciate.

Keep it positive. If there's been a recent death in the family, a nasty divorce or some other sort of strife, stay clear of getting into any of that. The exception would be if the bride or groom would like to acknowledge a deceased parent, relative or friend whom they wish could have been at the wedding (but is nevertheless there in spirit).

Be real with your emotions. If you can hardly wait for your 32-year-old daughter to finally get married and move out, don't be afraid to say so! OK, I'm kidding. But in all seriousness, don't be afraid to listen to your heart and express your sincere thoughts about how you're feeling (as in the scene from *Wedding Crashers*). This isn't a dry, corporate event – it's OK to get a little sentimental or to tell your sister how happy you are for her.

Skip the drama. Yes, weddings bring forth emotions. And yes, it's OK to be happy for the bridal couple and to wish them well. But it's not an excuse to be melodramatic, maudlin or overwrought with sentiment. Err on the side of caution with the length, humor and emotion you use in your speech.

Use a sounding board. If you're planning to use some material that you hope will be funny and inoffensive – but you're not 100% sure about it – check-in with a trusted "sounding board" that can offer an objective opinion as to its appropriateness. It's easy to get carried away with those funny yarns – but are they going to be appropriate for the wedding reception? Your spouse or best friend or perhaps even the bride or groom can tell you. Ditto for the schmaltzy stuff.

Check pronunciations. You wouldn't believe how many people mispronounce a name like "Haibeck" (it's of Norwegian descent and pronounced "high-beck"). If you risk saying someone's name wrong, check with them and spell it out phonetically in your speaking notes (as in "high-beck"). Then practice saying it prior to the reception.

Close with class. Conclude your toast on a positive note by wishing the couple well. You might want to offer some observations about the couple's strengths – as individuals and as a team. Be sincere in doing so – the time for being flip or satirical has now passed, and it's time to be warm and genuine. Remind yourself on that last cue card to invite the audience to stand and join you in your toast to the honoree(s).

Do it now. Make this process a priority in your life; material that you put together on the day of the wedding won't be nearly as well-considered as what you prepare several weeks prior to the wedding. You will also avoid the additional stress of having to prepare your material – and yourself – during the final days before the wedding. That time can be stressful enough without having to cope with the additional pressure of writing a last minute wedding speech.

For more tips on how to write your wedding tribute – and to view more samples of successful speeches – please visit my website at **WeddingToasts.com***. And if your toast is a big hit at the wedding, please feel free to send me a copy to post on that site (send text, photos or even video – my personal email address is tom@haibeck.com).*

*"There's nothing like a little liquid
courage to calm your nerves!"*

Dealing With Your Nervousness

Over the years, I've made hundreds of speeches, toasts and presentations. Once I get into the speech and become comfortable with my audience, I love it. But leading up to that point, I STILL get nervous about the prospect of public speaking.

That's particularly true in the case of a friend or family member's wedding reception. It seems there's a world of difference between addressing a room full of strangers and a room full of your friends, family and peers.

Perhaps it's the familiarity that can be so disconcerting – they know you and will continue to know you long after the wedding is over. If you blow it, they'll always be around to remind you of your moment of embarrassment.

On the other hand, you may never find a more supportive audience. These people like you and are on your side. They'll understand that the wedding isn't a full-blown Hollywood production and will gladly laugh with you at your own mistakes (providing you're also willing to share in that kind of humble, self-deprecating humor).

So don't take yourself too seriously; keep your cool and your sense of humor. On the following pages I've listed some tips that I've found helpful in dealing with my nervousness before addressing an audience. They're based on the specific techniques that I've developed for this purpose, and they do indeed work. I sincerely hope they help you as much as they've helped me over the years.

Do your homework. While a few lucky souls can speak brilliantly right off the cuff, most of us need to spend some time thinking about what we're going to say. That includes professional speakers, politicians, actors, comedians and talk show hosts. By following through with the tasks outlined in this book, you'll walk into that wedding feeling the kind of quiet confidence that comes from being thoroughly prepared and ready to do your best.

Get started early. One of the worst mistakes people make when asked to speak at a wedding is to procrastinate. If you fall into this trap, you might find that the pressure to perform will be overwhelming. On the other hand, if you're well-prepared in the weeks leading up to the wedding, you will enjoy the kind of quiet confidence I've just described (and you'll sleep a lot better during that period, as well).

Put the job in perspective. Ask yourself: What's the worst thing that could go wrong with my toast? I always imagine that the absolute worst thing that could happen is that I will lose my confidence, break down in tears in front of the audience, and have to run out of the room. Having imagined that scenario, I am always comforted to realize that's all I'm really afraid of – embarrassing myself in front of an audience.

I'll still live to play another game of golf, enjoy many more fine dinners with my family, and read a lot more good books. By putting the job in perspective and confronting my own worst fears about it, I always come to the realization that life will still go on for me, even if I fail miserably in speaking to an audience. That tends to reduce the pressure I may be feeling and boosts my confidence in going forward.

Harness your nervous energy. Some of the world's greatest actors and orators are regularly reduced to jelly before "going on," at which time they reclaim their calm and perform marvelously. Why? Because they have learned to use their nervous energy in sharpening their delivery, and focusing their concentration on the task at hand. If you're not somewhat nervous about your presentation, it may be a sign that you're inadequately prepared, and taking too casual an attitude towards your duties.

Visualize your success. Many of the world's top golfers spend time before each round visualizing their success on the golf course. They go to a quiet place, close their eyes and see themselves driving the ball 300 yards, pitching to within a few feet of the cup, and rolling in a crisp putt to make birdie. These golfers have learned to program their subconscious mind to record "success patterns" – and it works.

I suggest you try the same thing. Once you have prepared your presentation and rehearsed it a few times, try this exercise: Sit or lie down in a darkened room, take a few deep breaths, and try to relax your entire body. Then imagine yourself in front of the audience, speaking with confidence and enjoying your moment in the spotlight.

Run through your presentation in your mind's eye and visualize your success in delivering that presentation. Try to feel the glow of the audience as they warm to your delivery. See their smiling faces. Hear their laughter. Experience the burst of applause following your talk. Feel the pride – and the sense of relief – as you smile and walk back to your seat. Repeat this practice before you go to bed for at least five nights prior to the reception. Please note that I've recently produced a recording for this specific purpose – it's available at my website, **WeddingToasts.com**.

View the room where the reception will be held. Make an appointment with the catering manager or whomever is responsible for the facility in which the reception will be held and take a good look at the room where the event will unfold. I like to do this several weeks in advance, if possible. This helps me develop a much clearer picture of how the reception will "look" and aids in the visualization exercises I've just described.

Rehearse (aloud) in that same room. Students who suffer from severe anxiety about taking exams are often counseled to study in the room in which the examination will be given. That way, when it comes time to take the exam, they feel more at home with the entire process. Apply the same technique to your situation by rehearsing aloud in the reception facility. If possible, do so several weeks in advance of the wedding. That way, you will not only "see" the reception – you'll "hear" yourself at it.

Rehearse in the shower. Having a hot, steamy shower is a great way to relax. And the more experience you can get feeling relaxed while practicing your toast, the more natural and relaxed you will actually be come "show time."

Rehearse in front of a mirror. Stand before a mirror and deliver your toast. Notice how you look and get comfortable with yourself. Smile. Use hand gestures. Walk around. Own the room. See yourself being confident and successful.

Rehearse in your car. Put your commuting time to good use by practicing your toast on the way to or from work (but please also pay attention to your driving).

Rehearse in front of your spouse. If you feel comfortable in doing so, ask your spouse or partner to listen to your toast and offer feedback. They can be an excellent sounding board.

Video-tape your presentation. This can be a very powerful tool to help you improve your speaking and overall presentation skills. It will give you a much better sense of how you come across to the audience, and enable you to better identify your strengths and weaknesses.

Pre-tape your toast. Another option with videotape, however, is to engage a professional wedding videographer to help you record your toast in advance of the wedding. That tape can then be edited and shown at the wedding reception. If you're scared to death of public speaking, that might be a good option for you. To find a video pro in your area, check out WEVA.com (the Wedding & Event Videographers Association International).

Do some physical exercise on the day of the wedding. Go for a run, a walk, or a good swim on the morning of the wedding to help burn off some of your nervous energy. That exercise will also fuel your body with oxygen and feed your brain with endorphins (those chemicals that produce the famed "natural high" that runners get). A brisk workout will also help you feel more relaxed, healthy and clear (you'll also look better with those ruddy cheeks and bulging biceps).

Don't drink until after your program is finished. Many people like to loosen up with a few drinks before making a toast, but I would strongly discourage you from this practice. One or two drinks might be OK for a lot of people, but to go beyond that is to *rishk embarrashment* (such as Sandra Bullock's pie-eyed wedding day rampage in the movie, *"28 Days"*). And I've seen far too many people who planned to have one or two wind up having six or seven drinks (or more) in a failed effort to calm their nerves.

Most of us have been to a wedding that has been marred by the slurred, rambling speech of a drunken best man or an inebriated father of the bride – and it can be downright embarrassing for everyone involved.

THE CASE OF THE 90 MINUTE MARRIAGE

Another case in point: A few years ago, a story made headlines around the world about a marriage gone awry following a drunken toast at a wedding reception. According to a report in the London Daily Telegraph, a Manchester couple's marriage lasted all of 90 minutes following the groom's drunken diatribe in his toast to the bridesmaids. Enraged, the bride threw an ashtray at the groom, which prompted an ugly brawl that sent the groom to jail and the bride to a divorce lawyer. While that's obviously a rather extreme case, it's not at all unusual for an alcohol-induced rant to ruin an otherwise wonderful wedding.

Even a couple of drinks can have a pronounced effect on some people. If you're one of those people, and are concerned about the possibility of slurring your words or weaving your way to the podium, don't drink. You're going to be center stage, with all eyes upon you.

I would also suggest you drink sparingly the night before the wedding; again, speaking from experience, there's nothing worse than being horribly hung over while trying to speak intelligently at a wedding. We partied until the wee hours the night prior to one of the first weddings I was ever asked to speak at, and I can attest to the difficulties of trying to rise to the occasion when you're fighting to keep down your dinner. So put a cork in the bottle and give yourself a curfew the night before the wedding – you will be glad you did when it's time to make your toast.

Do some relaxation exercises before the reception. I like to spend some time just after the wedding ceremony, and right before the reception, doing some relaxation exercises (and no, I don't mean pumping back a half-dozen martinis). There are plenty of books and tapes that can teach you various relaxation techniques, and I find them very helpful in controlling my nervousness (try my relaxation tape at **WeddingToasts.com**).

Do some deep breathing. Just prior to your presentation, concentrate on taking several slow, deep breaths to relax your entire body. Take a few more deep breaths as you rise and approach the podium, position the microphone and lay down your notes. Continue to breathe as you address the audience.

Look for kind eyeballs in the audience. There are always certain people in an audience who will smile at you and listen attentively to what you are saying. Find those people early in your presentation and speak to them as much as you can. I've even gone so far in some presentations as to ask friends or family members in the audience to play a conscious role in offering those kindly eyes (and reassuring chuckles).

Your audience wants you to succeed. Nearly everyone has experienced some sort of embarrassing moment as a public speaker and can therefore relate to the nervousness you may be feeling. As a matter of fact, public speaking is the number one fear of the greatest number of people – ranking ahead of death by fire! You are by no means alone should you share that fear.

You're good at this. Chances are, the bride and groom selected you for this task because you're a good speaker. They have probably heard you speak to another group or watched you hold court with your friends and family. They obviously have a lot of confidence in your speaking abilities; no doubt others do as well. Use those votes of confidence to bolster your own.

Don't be afraid to laugh at yourself. Comedians like Jay Leno and Ellen Degeneres get some of their best laughs when they blow a routine and make fun of themselves for doing so. Have a good laugh at yourself, if necessary. It will break the ice and help you to release some anxiety in the process.

Study the pros. I recently attended a live taping of *The Late Show with David Letterman*. It was fabulous! I haven't laughed that hard in years, and the experience of watching Letterman get goofy with his guests, mug for the cameras, toy with the audience and kibitz with his band was something I'll never forget. It was educational, inspiring and a joy to watch – and those of us who are inclined towards performing tend to internalize and play off that kind of experience (just like a tennis fanatic becomes a better player by watching the pros). So go to a comedy club, an improv performance or a funny play and get into the spirit of live performance.

Take a course or join a Toastmasters group. I can't say enough about the value of breaking through your fear of public speaking. As mentioned in the introduction, it's always amazed me how kindergarten students can stand up in front of their classmates and deliver the most unabashed speeches about the items they bring for "show and tell." But somewhere along the road to adulthood, many of us lose that confidence and become terrified of speaking to an audience.

As you now know, I was such a specimen. In my youth, I could address a radio audience with relative ease, but when faced with that same audience live and in person, I could hardly utter my name, let alone a coherent speech.

That changed with my enrollment in the Dale Carnegie Course (**DaleCarnegie.com**). My life was quite literally transformed (at the tender age of 19), as I mastered my fear of public speaking and gained a confidence that extended into every area of my life. Millions of others will attest to that same experience, and I highly recommend it to anyone who has a fear of public speaking. Toastmasters also offers some excellent speaker development programs (see **ToastMasters.org**).

"Test, test, test, testicle ... oops, too loud, huh?"

Delivering Your Toast

You've reached zero hour. The wedding is now over, and the reception is just beginning. Guests are mingling easily, and everyone seems very happy. The bride looks radiant; the groom looks terrified; and their parents look ashen, as they mentally calculate the costs of this gala affair.

If you have done your homework to this point, you will be feeling very good about the evening. You have written a thoughtful, entertaining toast and rehearsed it enough that you feel completely comfortable with it. You have scoped out the room, prior to the reception, and feel at home in it. Your speaking notes are neatly written out on index cards, but you know your material so well by now that you will only need to occasionally glance at your notes while speaking.

Check in with the emcee or disc jockey to make sure everything is on track, and to confirm your spot in the order of toasts. If you haven't already done so, take a few moments to check the public address sytem, if there is one. The sound crew or disc jockey has probably already tested it to make sure it's working properly; but you might want to experiment a bit with the microphone prior to the guests entering the reception facility.

Better still, check the sound (if possible) well in advance of the reception (perhaps during the break between the ceremony and the wedding reception itself). That way, you can actually rehearse a little while using the microphone. Remember that the acoustics will change when the room is full of people, so be prepared to project your voice more if needed.

HOW TO USE A MICROPHONE

Different microphones demand different speaking styles. Some require you to hold the mic very close to your mouth (hand-held microphone); others, such as the lavalier or "lapel mic" pretty much allow you to forget about them. Ask the disc jockey, bandmaster or sound coordinator what type of microphone will be in use and how best to use it. Better yet, try to rehearse with the actual microphone you will be using.

Here are some general guidelines: If it's a hand-held version, plan to hold it two to three inches away from your mouth, and speak directly into it. Hold it steady – try not to sway or bob about, as your voice will fade in and out. If the microphone is attached to a lectern, be sure to raise or lower the microphone as necessary to ensure it's in speaking range (usually about a foot or so from your mouth).

Speak in your normal voice – there's no need to shout, as the microphone will naturally amplify your voice (although, as mentioned, you might need to project your voice somewhat if it's a noisy room).

PREPARE YOUR SPEAKING VOICE

If you're planning to make a longer toast that will see you speaking for more than two or three minutes, take some precautions for your throat and speaking voice. First of all, make sure you have a glass of water handy (as your throat can get very dried out after a few minutes of steady talking). But avoid drinking ice-cold beverages, as they will constrict your vocal chords. Warm water or tea are better choices (avoid milk). Plan to pop a lozenge just prior to your toast.

Make sure you have something to eat during dinner – you will need the energy for later on (if your toast is after dinner). Do not drink more than a glass of wine at dinner. Better still, don't drink at all.

Skim through your speaking notes during dinner to refresh your memory about what you're going to say. If your notes are on index cards, you can easily store them in your jacket pocket. Carry a copy of the agenda so you'll know when it's your turn.

CHECK YOUR APPEARANCE

Look your best – and try to make a quick trip to the washroom prior to your toast to check your appearance and take care of any other required business. If you're planning to do a quick relaxation exercise prior to your toast, the washroom (or an empty office or meeting room near by) will provide you with the needed privacy (and silence) for that purpose.

Make sure you know where (in the room) your toast is to take place. If you're using a hand-held microphone, stand directly behind or adjacent to the bride and groom (or the subject of your toast). Another option is to ask the couple to stand next to you (but not if you're delivering a long speech).

Remember to have a glass of wine, champagne or a soft drink handy prior to your toast. The beverage you choose should be poured into a proper wine glass or champagne flute prior to your toast. Carry that glass with you to your toasting place.

LECTERNS WORK BEST

My preference is to have a lectern in place for all of the speakers to use in making their toasts. That way, they can easily lay out their notes (rather than trying to hold a microphone in one hand while juggling their speaking notes in the other hand).

As you stand and walk to the podium (or upon reaching the podium), try smiling at the audience (and the bride and groom) before saying anything. You'll be amazed at what a sincere smile can do in winning people over from the start.

Watch your stance and posture. Avoid rocking back and forth or the temptation to check if your fly is open. Take a deep breath. Feel yourself relax. Look for those special people in the audience with those kind eyeballs. And begin your talk.

Try to avoid the tendency to rush through your toast. While it's certainly important to keep it relatively brief, it's also important to relax and take your time as you deliver your toast. Speak loudly enough so everyone can hear you (but don't shout). Have fun – and please let me know how it goes (tom@haibeck.com).

The Role of a Wedding MC

In many parts of the world, it's customary for the best man to also serve as emcee for the wedding reception. That's not always the case – if that individual has a bad case of stage fright or simply doesn't feel equipped for that role, another family member (or friend of the family) might take on that role.

Another option is to hire a professional mobile entertainer (disc jockey) to serve as both emcee for the reception and as entertainment director for the dance and festivities to follow. But regardless of who takes on role of Master of Ceremonies for the wedding reception, I am absolutely convinced of the need for it.

A wedding reception falls into the category of "special event" – and as any special event planner will tell you, an event needs a Master of Ceremonies. Someone has to step forward and take charge of the proceedings. They need to work with the couple well in advance of the reception to determine an agenda which clearly identifies how the event is to unfold, the timing for each segment of it, who is to speak or offer a toast, when that is to happen, how they are to be introduced, plus all the other subtle details that are so often overlooked at a wedding reception.

In fairness, planning a wedding reception is an entirely new experience for most couples. They simply don't have the knowledge or experience to know what needs to be done, nor the time to properly research and put together a great event. But in the time it takes to read the next few pages of this book, most anyone can learn how to plan and organize a wedding reception that runs smoothly and proves fun and entertaining for everyone.

But aside from the mechanics of the event, a good emcee can add needed warmth and personality to a wedding reception. They can help ensure it meets expectations, whether that be a classy, formal affair or a more relaxed and informal occasion. They can also help ensure that those embarrassing 37-minute frat house rambles never occur (they get the hook).

AMATEUR OR PROFESSIONAL MC?

For some people, all of those details will be expertly handled by a professional wedding planner, who will in turn enlist the services of a professional disc jockey. That's a great option – if you can afford it. But the fact is, many people can't.

Let's be clear: A professional DJ can do wonders for a wedding reception dance (following the dinner). That's what they're good at – and they can put together an excellent show with very little advance preparation. But if you expect them to take on dual roles as both MC for the reception dinner AND as DJ for the dance that follows, you might be disappointed.

Most professional disc jockeys simply won't devote the time it takes to properly prepare to serve as emcee – unless you pay them an additional fee. Time is money in their business. Don't expect them to invest the extra hours unless you are prepared to pay them for those additional services.

Again, if you can afford to do so, great (most DJs will do an excellent job as MC if properly paid) If not, I strongly recommend you enlist the best man, a close friend or a relative to work with you in doing what is outlined in this book. Trust me: Based on my experience – and that of the 100,000+ who have bought this book – a close friend or relative can do a first-class job in emceeing a wedding.

The other key advantage that a close friend or relative has over the professional DJ (in acting as MC) is the fact that he or she is truly connected with the couple. A favorite uncle of the bride or a close friend of the groom can bring a unique blend of knowledge and personalized experience to the wedding reception that simply can't be duplicated by a professional.

They are authentic – they share a very real connection with the couple, their families and their friends. And that connection will usually translate into a much warmer, more moving and far more intimate wedding reception dinner than one that is hosted by a paid professional.

THE HONOR OF SERVING AS EMCEE
A close friend or family member is also uniquely motivated to serve as emcee. Why? Because they have an ongoing relationship with those in attendance. And believe me, no one wants to fail miserably in front of a group of people that they will continue to see at family dinners and events for many years to come.

This isn't just another gig for them – it's an honor and a privilege to help some very special people in their lives commemorate one of the biggest days in their lives.

It's also an opportunity for them to shine. While the spotlight should indeed be on the bride and groom, the wedding emcee will be front and centre at the podium. That has a way of galvanizing the attention of that particular individual – and often inspires him or her to devote an inordinate amount of time and effort in preparing for their role.

That usually translates into a superb performance at the wedding itself (providing, of course, you give them a copy of this book and ask them to carefully study it and do what is recommended).

CHOOSING A WEDDING EMCEE
First of all, choose someone who has the confidence to address a large audience. Not everyone can do that, and if the person isn't comfortable in that role, they shouldn't be asked to take it on. Look for someone who has led business meetings or spoken to large groups.

Next on the list would be someone who has presence – the ability to command and hold an audience's attention. The primary role of an emcee is to lead the audience through the event – and in order to do so, the emcee must be able to take charge of the proceedings and keep the event moving.

I would also look for someone who is clear-headed, organized and able to think on their feet. There are typically a lot of details to be considered in the planning and execution of a wedding reception, and the emcee needs to be able to work with the bride and groom to help ensure their vision (of the reception) is carried out. They also need to be able to improvise a bit if things go a little off track.

A sense of humor helps – but is not entirely necessary. Just because someone is funny does NOT mean they will be a great emcee. The other qualities I've mentioned are far more important (public speaking experience; presence; clarity; ability to be organized and to think on his/her feet).

MORE ON HUMOR

I have discussed the topic of humor in previous sections of the book that deal with making a wedding toast, and the same principles apply for those who serve as emcee. If you're not funny, don't try to be. If you are funny, don't overdo it.

Keep it clean – before telling a joke or using a one-liner, ask yourself if your grandmother would be offended by it (as weddings typically involve a wide cross-section of guests). Watch your language. Avoid "insider humor" that only a few people will appreciate. Road trip stories, events at the stag party and intimate details about the groom's hair transplant procedure are strictly off-limits. Also be careful not to embarrass or up-stage others asked to speak or make a toast.

THE FINAL DECISION

To summarize: If you have the budget and are more comfortable going with a professional emcee, do so. The advantage in doing so is that you know the person at the microphone has the knowledge and experience to competently emcee the reception. But if budget is an issue and/or you would prefer to add a more genuine, familial element to your wedding, ask the best man, a friend or family member to serve as emcee. Just give them a copy of this book and work with them on the steps that follow. If you *are* the emcee, let's get started!

The Duties of a Wedding MC

If you have been asked to emcee a wedding reception, congratulations. It's a great honor to do so – and the the experience in serving as a wedding emcee could prove to be one of the most gratifying experiences of your life.

Why? Because the experience of presiding over an event (such as a wedding reception) that turns out to be a roaring success (with you at the helm) can be incredibly empowering. When guests tell you afterwards that you did an amazing job and that everyone had such a good time, it will do wonders for your confidence.

You might find yourself being asked to emcee other weddings and special events (which could then lead to professional opportunities as a speaker or emcee). That's precisely what happened to me – and it was all the result of being asked to emcee my buddy's wedding many, many years ago.

But the most rewarding part of serving as emcee (and doing a great job) is the look of delight on the faces of the bride and groom (and their families). This is their day – and it may indeed be the biggest day in their entire lives.

An effective wedding emcee can make an enormous difference on that special day. And if the duties of being Master of Ceremonies have fallen on your shoulders, I encourage you to take the role seriously and do what it takes to help make it a great event. You want it to be remembered for all the right reasons – and to do so, you're going to need to put some time and effort into your role as emcee. It's not that difficult – if you take the time to prepare.

GETTING STARTED

So what does a "wedding emcee" actually do? Simply stated, your job is to preside over the wedding reception. Just as a meeting needs a chairman, so, too, does a wedding reception need a host or emcee. Someone has to be responsible for making sure the show gets on the road and stays on the road.

The bride and groom have probably chosen you for the job because you have a talent for keeping things under control and a certain amount of confidence in assuming that role. The couple no doubt has enough on their minds without having to worry about the reception itself and so they have asked you to take charge. And that's exactly what you should do – take charge!

Now please don't confuse this with taking charge of the wedding itself. The bride and her mother will have plenty to say about that and will have spent many hours planning and coordinating the day. Depending upon what format the reception takes, you may be required to direct guests to dinner, introduce the head table, read messages from those unable to attend, achnowledge special guests, deliver a toast, smooth over a few rough spots, introduce other speakers and coordinate the traditional cake-cutting ceremony.

You may also be asked to help plan the reception program, and so be prepared to offer suggestions and guidance if necessary. The next chapter offers a sample agenda and some notes to follow in planning the wedding reception. But please remember at all times to be sensitive towards the wishes of the wedding couple and their parents — it is, after all, their special day.

I would encourage you to read through other sections of this book to help prepare you for The Big Day. The same advice on getting ready to make a toast is readily applicable to your role as emcee.

Start early. Do your research. Get to know the people you've been asked to introduce. Make notes. Get organized. Rehearse. Time yourself. Have a look at the room (or area) in which the wedding reception will take place (and rehearse there if possible). Learn to use a microphone. Do some relaxation and visualization exercises. Don't drink until after your duties are complete. Be careful in using humor. And prepare an agenda (next chapter).

*"So before we discuss what you want,
let's discuss my vision for the reception."*

Planning the Reception

Like any party, wedding receptions take many forms. Some are staged in elaborate ballrooms. Others unfold in someone's backyard. Dinner may be served for several hundred guests. Or a few close friends might gather around a bottle of champagne.

Whatever format the reception takes will be determined by the overall budget for the wedding, the number of people invited, where it is held, and the personal preferences of the wedding couple and their families.

If it's a large wedding, with 50 or more people and a formal sit-down dinner, I would strongly recommend that the people who are planning it prepare an event agenda. An event agenda is to a wedding reception what a script is to a movie. It's a written document that describes precisely how the event is to unfold, the timing for each element of it and who is responsible for each of those elements.

As any wedding or event planner will tell you, an event agenda is critically important to the success of the wedding reception. It will quite literally ensure that everyone involved in the reception is on the same page – and that includes the people who have been asked to speak or make toasts.

I've included a sample wedding reception agenda on page 79. Please note that this is merely a sample agenda; yours may be much different. The important thing is to work with the couple (and their families) in planning each phase of the event and to get it down on paper.

THE EVENT AGENDA

I have provided a sample agenda (next page) for your reference in planning a "sit-down" reception. Details on each part of this particular agenda follow in later chapters (along with some thoughts on how to make it all come together).

Please remember, though, that this is simply a suggested agenda; there is no universally recognized "etiquette" to govern a wedding reception, so do what works best for the bridal couple, their families and you.

Once completed, the agenda should identify who is involved and list the order of events, with a time-frame for their completion. Start at the beginning of the event and work your way through to the end. I've included a handy list of questions for you to ask the bride and her mother (page 37) that will help you through that process.

The final agenda should be limited to one page (as in the sample) and distributed to:

- The bridal couple and their parents
- Other key decision-makers, such as the wedding planner
- The individuals in the wedding party
- The caterer (or whomever is responsible for dinner)
- The bartender and/or head waiter
- The person who will offer a blessing before dinner
- People who have been asked to make toasts
- The wedding DJ and/or entertainers
- The photographer/videographer
- Anyone else with a key role in the wedding reception

Preparing an agenda and getting everyone a copy in advance of the reception might seem like a lot of work. But if all the key players know what's going to happen before it all starts happening (and are aware of their particular roles and responsibilities) – the event itself will go a lot smoother.

And you, as the Master of Ceremonies, will do a much better job of orchestrating it!

AGENDA FOR HUDSON / O'FLYNN WEDDING
The Fairmont Plaza Hotel – August 21, 2009

6:55 Guests to be seated before wedding party enters. MC to introduce himself, welcome guests on behalf of couple.

7:00 MC to ask guests to rise and applaud bridal party as they enter the room. After that, ask Minister Reeves to say grace.

7:05 MC to invite guests to help themselves to buffet dinner, starting with tables to his immediate left.

7:15 MC to remind guests of alternatives to clinking spoons onglasses to encourage Bride and Groom to kiss each other.

7:40 While dessert is being served, MC to read messages from guests unable to attend, introduce guests who traveled long distances, acknowledge other special guests.

7:45 MC to call upon Ed Bergen, friend of the Hudson family, to give Toast to the Bride.

7:55 MC to introduce Best Man – Dave Johnson, who offers a toast to the new couple.

8:00 MC to introduce Groom – Ryan O'Flynn, who responds to toasts, thanks Bride's parents/wedding party, offers Toast to the Bridesmaids (and tells wife he loves her).

8:05 MC to introduce Father of Bride – Fred Hudson, who welcomes new son/thanks guests for attending.

8:10 MC relates a few more humorous stories about Bride and Groom, calls upon couple to cut cake.

8:25 After cake is cut, MC to introduce entertainment, encourage guests to dance and enjoy themselves.

11:00 MC to invite single women to gather in centre of dance floor for bouquet toss by Bride; garter toss by Groom.

*"Here's to hoping their marriage
lasts past the honeymoon!"*

Preparing the Agenda

The sample agenda on the previous page lists the approximate times for specific events, the order in which they will happen, and who is responsible for doing what.

It's the same kind of agenda that I would put together if I were planning a major event or reception for one of my public relations clients. It provides structure for the event and ties together all the various elements that will go into it. For just as a movie needs a script, an event needs an agenda.

An event agenda also provides a way to create written agreement amongst the various parties as to what will happen at the reception, the order in which they will happen, approximate times for completion of each key segment of the event and confirmation as to who is to be responsible for the various elements of the program (e.g. "Uncle Charlie to make the Toast to the Bride at 8:30 PM").

Of all the recommendations made in this book, preparing an event agenda ranks amongst the most important, in my opinion. As mentioned, these kind of details need to be thoroughly discussed and resolved well in advance of the wedding reception, when everyone's mind is clear and their attention is focused.

Advance planning also enables you to bring together the myriad of parties that may be involved in the reception, from the families themselves to the various professionals involved (caterers, disc jockey, band, etc.). Trying to chase down everyone the day before the event will be difficult, at best.

Also, having been through a bad case of pre-wedding jitters, I can tell you that the wedding party will have enough on its collective mind in the days leading up to the wedding without having to worry about the timing for Uncle Charlie's toast.

HOLD A PLANNING MEETING

If you can all meet face-to-face, do so. But if you live in a different city than the bride and groom (and others involved in the event), hold your planning sessions over the phone, and follow-up with everyone via e-mail. And if you are reading this book and starting to feel like the other people involved should be made more aware of the importance of this process, you might suggest they purchase an eBook version of *"Wedding Toasts Made Easy"* from my website at **WeddingToasts.com**. It will make an enormous difference having everyone on the same page, so to speak.

As mentioned, the sample agenda is simply a suggested sequence of events; the bride and her mother may want you to do certain things in another order, and you may be more comfortable adding or deleting certain elements from your program. Whatever you decide to do in your role as emcee, make sure it is written down, that it receives proper approval, and that other key people involved in the reception program know what's going on.

The timing of events is particularly important for the emcee. You must know when the refreshments will be served so that guests' glasses are filled when it's time to make toasts. You must also know what time the program should start and end, when the entertainers are scheduled to perform, what time the bride and groom would like to leave and when guests should leave if the hall must be cleared by a certain time.

THE TIMING FOR TOASTS

If possible, I would encourage you to keep the reception program itself (that is, the speeches and toasts that follow the dinner or refreshments) to a maximum of a half hour. Unless all speakers are particularly eloquent or entertaining, to go beyond twenty or thirty minutes will probably strain the audience's attention. Suggest that individuals offering toasts keep their speeches to five minutes or less (but be tactful in doing this).

Keep your watch before you at all times during the reception, along with your agenda. If the program starts to drag or goes off-course for some reason, try to cut down on your own material. Similarly, be prepared to offer some "fill" if the program goes too fast (a couple of jokes or stories, one-liners or anecdotes about the bride and groom).

Be flexible. Unexpected changes can often alter the course of events for even the best-planned weddings, and it's your job to try to smooth things over when they happen (but remember that the "bloopers" or "out-takes" section of most DVDs contain some of the funniest and most spontaneous humor to be found in the entire production; so do your best to relax and not get flustered or upset if things start to go awry).

Let's re-visit the reception agenda now with some thoughts on putting it all together.

THE BRIDE & GROOM'S ENTRANCE

Your first duty may be to ask the wedding guests to stand and welcome members of the bridal party as they make their entrance into the reception area. At some weddings, the guests are expected to applaud the bridal party's entrance (if that's the case, be sure to start the applause). Ask the guests to be seated once the bridal party has been seated.

WELCOME TO GUESTS

A good way to start the program is to welcome guests on behalf of the wedding couple and to then introduce yourself. *"On behalf of the new Mr. and Mrs.* _____, *I'd like to welcome you to this joyous occasion. My name is* _____, *and I'm ...."* (give your relationship to the wedding party — friend, relative, parole officer). If it's a stand-up reception, call upon the guests to gather around the wedding couple before starting.

THE TOAST TO THE NEW COUPLE

You may want to offer a toast to the new couple at this point, but keep it short and sweet. *"Ladies and gentlemen, please join me in toasting the new Mr. and Mrs.* _____*."*

THE BLESSING

Ask the person who is to say grace to proceed. *"I'd now like to call upon* _____ *to say grace."*

THE DINNER

If the dinner is being served by the catering staff, there is probably no need to make any further announcements until dessert comes. If the dinner is buffet style, you may want to announce which tables are to help themselves first:*"Ladies and gentlemen, please help yourselves to the buffet, starting with the tables to my immediate right."* In some cases, the catering staff may want to say something about the dinner as well, so check with them beforehand. You may also want to acknowledge the caterers after dinner with a round of applause. Your goal is to generate as much postive energy as possible in that room!

THE CLINKING OF SPOONS ON GLASSES

Ask the bride and groom if they would like you to make an announcement about this practice, which signals them to kiss one another. Sometimes it can get tiresome, and the wedding couple may want you to ask the guests to do something else.

For example, you might invite guests (or the table at which they are sitting) to come forward during the dinner and sing a song with the word "love" in it (rather than clink glasses). This can be a lot of fun, as it encourages the guests (individually or in a group) to let their hair down and get into the act. It will also help break the ice for the toasts and for your presentation.

Another option: Ask couples in the audience to kiss, with the proviso that the bride and groom must kiss each other in the same manner. The contortions and uhm ... "displays of affection" for the bride and groom to have to mimic can leave the audience in stitches.

JOKES/ANNOUNCEMENTS DURING DINNER

You might tell a few humorous stories during dinner to keep the evening moving. In my experience, however, it's usually best to let the guests enjoy their dinner and chat amongst themselves.

MESSAGES/SPECIAL GUESTS

I like to take care of this part of the program while dessert is being served. The messages can make for some fairly easy material to get a laugh (especially if you make up a couple of humorous ones – suggestion: *"Congratulations Sheila on your big day. We'll miss you. Signed, Bob ... Ed ... Tony ... Mike ... Rupert ... Eduardo ... and Carleton the doorman."*)

The practice of acknowledging special guests (elderly relatives, people who have traveled a long way to attend the wedding) also helps to focus the audience's attention on themselves rather than on you. This can help relieve some of the pressure you may be feeling in starting the program. It's also an excellent means of winning the audience's support and attention.

RE-INTRODUCE YOURSELF

When you introduced yourself at the very start of the program, you didn't go into much detail other than to state your relationship to the wedding couple (e.g. *"I'm Mary's Uncle"*). You might want to re-introduce yourself at this point with a phrase such as *"in case you've forgotten who I am"* or *"you're probably wondering all about me."*

I would recommend doing this because: a) audiences like to know something about the person they're listening to, and b) if you plan to make any humorous but disparaging remarks about someone else in the wedding party, they'll probably go over better if you've poked a bit of fun at yourself first. If you do re-introduce yourself at this point, though, keep it light and brief. And if you don't feel comfortable doing this, don't.

INTRODUCE THE HEAD TABLE

Wedding guests always enjoy knowing a bit of background on each member of the wedding party – and the wedding party will feel honored to be acknowledged with a brief introduction. Start at one end of the table and introduce each of the bridesmaids and groomsmen before re-introducing the wedding couple. If you have done your homework, you will have chatted with each member of the wedding party before the wedding to learn where they are from, what they do for a living, how they met the wedding couple – that kind of thing. This information can make for some excellent comedy material by embellishing it a bit or by pointing out some of the quirks or eccentricities of each individual.

TOAST TO THE BRIDE

Now that your audience has been introduced to the head table guests, it's time to call upon people to make a few toasts. The first toast is always to the bride and/or new couple and is often made by the best man, a close friend or a relative (this person may or may not be sitting at the head table). Make sure everyone's glass is filled before calling upon the person who is to make this toast.

THE GROOM'S RESPONSE

It's customary for the groom to respond to the toast made to his new bride by offering his own toast to any or all of the following: the bridesmaids, the mother of the bride, parents of the bride, his own parents; other special people. While introducing the groom, though, you might want to tell a few humorous stories about him and perhaps his new wife. Or, you can leave this until after the groom has made his toast(s).

OTHER TOASTS

If there are other toasts to be made, make sure you know about them in advance, and that they are on the agenda. When introducing people who are about to make a toast, keep the introduction short and sweet: *"I'd now like to call upon Mr. Bert Ostlund, who is a friend of the groom, to offer a toast to the bridesmaids."*

In my experience, it's a good idea for the emcee to introduce each person making a toast. What often happens is that once the first toast is made, the audience continues to buzz and a second toast can easily be drowned out (especially if the person making the toast doesn't have a strong presence or speaking voice). Intros also provide a nice "bridge" between toasts.

However, if a significant number of people are going to make toasts (more than four or five), let each person introduce him/herself (to avoid too much back and forth between them and you as emcee).

FATHER OF THE BRIDE THANKS GUESTS

The bride's father might want to thank all guests at this point for attending the wedding; he may also want to say a couple of nice things about his new son-in-law (this is strictly optional, but it's a classy thing to do – even if you have to lie).

THE CAKE-CUTTING CEREMONY

The toasts and formal part of the program are usually followed by the traditional cake-cutting ceremony. Invite the couple to cut the cake, and those with cameras to come forward to take pictures. Make sure the event photographer(s) are fully prepared for the historic moment when knife meets icing.

ANNOUNCE THE EVENING'S ENTERTAINMENT

If a band, disc jockey or other entertainers have been booked to perform, introduce them and let them take over from there. A good way to make the transition is for the band or disc jockey to then introduce the couple's selected music for their first dance.

THE BOUQUET TOSS

Later in the evening, you may announce the bouquet toss by inviting the single women to gather in the middle of the dance floor to try to catch the bouquet thrown by the bride. You may also invite all bachelors to catch the bride's garter, as thrown by the groom. Confirmed bachelors might also be invited to stay clear of the toss.

THE SEND-OFF

After the bride and groom have returned to the reception in their going-away clothes, you may want to announce their "send-off" by asking the guests to gather around them, wish them good luck and send them on their way by throwing rice and confetti. On the other hand, the bride and groom may wish to quietly slip away without having a big fuss made out of their departure – discuss this with them prior to the reception.

Questions to Ask the Bride & Her Mother

Now that you have learned the importance of advance planning and the need to nail down an agenda, here are some questions to review with the decision-makers (who are usually the bride and her mother).

Try to go through these at least a month before the wedding (if possible) to give everyone time to do what's required. The answers to these questions will ultimately help determine how the reception will unfold and what it is expected of you – so take your time, give them some careful thought and make sure everyone is clear on what gets decided.

I strongly recommend that you follow-up this meeting with a written summary of your understanding of what was decided (just some point form notes about key things). You should also prepare a detailed copy of the actual agenda (see sample).

If you're not great at taking notes or writing summaries, ask someone else in the group to do so. I can't stress enough the importance of having a written record of what gets decided and what the actual agenda will look like. Believe me, things get lost in translation, people forget what was agreed upon and confusion too often reigns in the days leading up to the wedding. So get it down on paper – then send copies to the key decision-makers for the wedding (along with a copy of the agenda to those will be play key parts in the reception).

QUESTIONS TO ASK THE BRIDE & HER MOTHER:

1. Where will the reception be held?

2. What is the actual address of the reception venue? Phone number? Fax number? E-mail address? Contact person?

3. Does the facility have a website (to preview)?

4. Is it difficult to find – will you need directions on how to get there?

5. What time are you expected to be at the reception?

6. Can you gain access to the reception venue well in advance of the wedding day (to preview, rehearse and get a sense of how the event will flow)?

7. Who will be the contact person for the MC during the wedding reception (the bride or her mother or someone else)?

8. How many guests are expected?

9. Is it a stand-up reception or a sit-down dinner?

10. If it is a sit-down dinner, will it be buffet style or will guests be served their meals?

11. What time will dinner and/or refreshments be served?

12. Who will be responsible for asking guests to be seated?

13. Should serving staff (or others) be asked to help move the guests from the reception area into the dining area?

14. Will the bridal party make a special entrance that needs to be announced?

15. If so, who will cue the MC that the bridal party is ready to make their entrance?

16. Once the head table is seated, should the MC offer a toast to the new couple or introduce members of the wedding party?

17. Is there to be a blessing before dinner? If so, who will offer the blessing?

18. Are there any special announcements to be made about the dinner or the refreshments? (For example, do guests need to be directed to the buffet or to the open bar, etc.)

19. What does the couple want said about the traditional clinking of glasses during dinner to prompt them to kiss each other?

20. Will there be a public address system?

21. Will there be an audio technician or disc jockey at the reception to operate the sound system?

22. When would be a good time to do a pre-reception sound check?

23. Will there be a podium?

24. Will the MC speak from a stage or at the head table?

25. Where will the MC sit through dinner?

26. Where will the toasts/speeches be delivered from?

27. Does anyone require a hand-held microphone? Other audio-visual tools (for example, a laptop and projector?)

28. Does anyone who will be making a toast need some extra help with their toast or a briefing on the use of a microphone?

29. At what point should the main program begin?

30. Who will toast the new bride/new couple?

31. Does the groom (and/or the bride) want to respond to that toast?

32. Who will toast the bridesmaids?

33. Are there any other toasts to be made?

34. Does the father of the bride want to say anything?

35. Does the father of the groom want to say anything?

36. Does anyone else want to say anything?

37. Are there any special family traditions to be upheld?

38. Are there any special guests to be acknowledged?

39. Will there be any special e-mails to be read from well-wishers unable to attend?

40. If so, who will provide them to the MC?

41. What are the names of the head-table guests?

42. Would it be appropriate to offer some background information on each person in introducing them?

43. If so, would it be appropriate to contact each individual and conduct a brief interview prior to the wedding? Contact info?

44. Is anyone's name difficult to pronounce?

45. How would you describe the audience? Elderly and conservative? Religious? Young and hip? A mixture?

46. Is anyone particularly sensitive about humor?

47. Is there to be a disc jockey, band or other performers?

48. If so, how is the transition to be made from MC to DJ/band?

49. Who is to announce the cake-cutting?

50. Who will announce the first dance?

51. Will there be a bouquet toss – and if so, when?

52. Will there be a garter scramble – and if so, when?

53. At what time do the bride and groom want to leave?

54. How will the bride and groom be sent off?

55. Are there any other announcements that need to be made?

56. By what time must all guests leave?

57. Will impaired guests be offered safe transporation home?

58. Is there anything else we need to review?

59. Who needs to be copied on the agenda or summary?

"I got it, I got it...!"

Duties of the Best Man

So what does a "Best Man" actually do? Well, if we go to the very essence of the role, it's to stand up at a wedding to support the guy getting married, and to witness the vows between bride and groom.

The best man and the maid of honour are also typically required to sign the wedding license to legally attest that the marriage has, in fact, taken place.

But being a best man means much more than that. It is one of the greatest affirmations of friendship between men, and to be chosen for the role is another one of life's great honours.

It's a big deal – and aside from the significance of the designation itself, the role carries with it some very important responsibilities (more on that later). Treat that role with the respect it deserves, and vow to be the best friend you can be to the groom as he walks the plank ..... I mean his path to marriage.

Getting married is ranked as one of life's most stressful events and in most cases, the groom can use all the help he can get. In my opinion, the most important thing you can do in your role as best man is to simply "be there" for the guy taking his vows. In my case, the best man at our wedding played a crucial role in helping me prepare for The Big Day (and I was, shall we say, a "high maintenance" groom-to-be).

We talked regularly during the period leading up to the wedding, and he listened to my concerns and shared my excitement. He accompanied me to the various engagement parties given in our honour; made sure I survived the bachelor party I'll never remember; took me for a walk just prior to the wedding ceremony to get some fresh air and help ease my nerves; sat with me in the minister's office prior to the wedding and told jokes while I paced back and forth; and generally provided the kind of friendship and support a guy needs leading up to the wedding.

(He also called our hotel room at 3:00 a.m. on the night of the wedding to inquire about our progress in consummating the marriage, but that's a whole other story).

CHOOSING THE BEST MAN

It is most often a close friend or brother who is asked to be the best man – although I've been to one wedding at which the groom's father served as best man and another where a female friend of the groom was given the honours (she even wore a tuxedo, which was a cute touch. Her suggestion that we hold the bachelor party at a day spa got vetoed, however).

Now to the mechanics of the role. If we were to write a job description for the best man, it would describe a series of duties to be undertaken before, during and after the wedding to help ensure everything proceeds smoothly (and the groom shows up for the wedding). That job might include all or many of the responsibilities listed on the next page (the duties vary somewhat, depending upon the type of wedding and the expectations of the couple and their families).

BRIEFING THE BEST MAN

Frankly, most guys who are asked to serve as best man have no idea about what is expected of them in that role. Therefore, they tend to appreciate having someone explain those responsibilities prior to the wedding.

That task is probably best handled by the groom – after all, he's chosen his best man and can probably best describe the role he envisions for him (but again, most grooms are also clueless about anything to do with weddings, which is probably a good thing). Another option is for someone else involved in the wedding (father of the groom, for example) to take the best man to lunch and give him a copy of this book.

Here's a list of some of the official duties of a best man (as originally offered by Dear Abby and enhanced by yours truly):

- Volunteering to help the bride's mother or other wedding organizers as needed;

- Accompanying the groom to the engagement parties and other events leading up to the wedding;

- Helping the groom coordinate the formalwear fittings (if required) for the guys in the wedding party;

- Suggesting to the other guys in the wedding party that they pay for their own formalwear rental charges;

- Heading up the organizing committee for the bachelor party, including the collection of funds to pay for the party itself (the groom shouldn't have to bear any of those costs);

- Ensuring the safe transportation of all guests at the bachelor party (if liquor is to be involved);

- Stepping in as necessary to help ensure the groom doesn't endure too much abuse at the bachelor party (seriously, alcohol poisoning can be deadly, and to force the groom to drink ridiculous amounts of alcohol is to risk serious consequences – or at least, a big mess to clean up);

- Either separately (or with the ushers) providing a special gift to the groom to help commemorate the event and the special friendship it involves (a framed picture of the group at the bachelor party, signed by all the guys, is a nice touch);

- Attending the rehearsal dinner and being available to help with any last minute arrangements for the wedding itself;

- Making the arrangements to transport the groom to the wedding (I suggest you pick him up, handcuff him to the steering wheel and drive him to the church);

- If necessary, helping the groom get dressed for the wedding (it's amazing how difficult it can be to button those fancy shirts that come with the tuxedo rental – especially when you're getting married in an hour);

- Making sure the ushers have their proper attire and that they appear on time at the wedding ceremony;

- Instructing the ushers on the proper procedure for greeting guests and escorting them to their seats (family and friends of the bride on the left side of the church, family and friends of the groom on the right side);

- Presenting the clergy with the envelope containing the fee for the ceremony;

- Sitting with the groom prior to the wedding (the best man does not help with the ushering process). This can be one of *the* most stressful times of all for the groom, so plan to be there with him during his final moments of freedom ... I mean bachelorhood;

- Reviving the groom should he faint when the minister calls for you to head to the altar;

- Standing proud next to him during the wedding ceremony, acting as a witness to the vows and in the signing of the official marriage license;

- Taking possession of the wedding ring(s) prior to the ceremony, and providing them to the minister at the time during the ceremony that they are required;

- Ensuring a bottle of chilled champagne (or their beverage of choice) awaits the bride and groom in the limousine (or other mode of transportation) from the wedding ceremony to the wedding reception venue;

- Mingling with the guests at the reception and being available to assist with last minute errands, announcements or other logistics as required;

- Offering a Toast to the Groom or a first toast to the new couple; assisting with the ceremonies by introducing other speakers, if required;

- Breaking up any bar fights that might erupt between rival in-laws or motorcycle gangs on the guest list;

- Gathering up the wedding gifts and transporting them for safe storage during and after the wedding (this is important – there are actually thieves out there who have been known to target weddings and steal the gifts that so often get stored in unlocked rooms in hotels or meeting facilities);

- Helping the groom, as needed, in packing his vehicle, confirming hotel reservations, or driving him and his new wife to the airport or hotel;

- Attending the gift-opening party the next day (if one is planned);

- Ensuring the ushers and other groomsmen return their formalwear rentals on time;

- Helping out as needed before, during and after the wedding.

BE THE MAIN CONTACT ON WEDDING DAY

Here's another little tip that can prove invaluable if something goes awry on the day of the wedding. Provide all of the key wedding vendors (the photographer; videographer; florist; chauffeur; caterer; disc jockey; band leader; etc.) with your cell phone number and tell them to call you in case of emergency. Then, plan to keep your cell phone on silent vibrate and be ready to respond if one of those key suppliers gets lost, blows a tire or some other unforeseen disaster occurs.

BE THE BEST, BEST MAN YOU CAN BE

As you can see, the best man's responsibilities extend far beyond just showing up at the wedding and witnessing the vows. It is indeed a lot to take on – but it's also a tremendous honour to be asked to serve as best man. Bear that in mind – and know that your support will be critically important to the success of the wedding (and the mental health of the groom).

So be there for your buddy before, during and after The Big Day – and don't forget to shortsheet his bed.

*"If you thought I was great at the wedding,
wait 'til we get to the honeymoon!"*

A Treasury of Wedding Quips, Quotes & Humour

The following pages list dozens of suggested quips, one-liners and famous quotations for you to consider in preparing your wedding toast or speech. Feel free to use them as needed.

Some are romantic. Others are philosophical. And many are satirical. Use them at your discretion – and please note that I have tried to provide a balance between the male and female-oriented comedy material on the subject of marriage (given today's need for balance and gender equality).

Keep it light and remember how important it is to laugh at ourselves and to see the humour in life (including marriage). For just as Hollywood excess is a constant source of amusement at Academy Awards presentations, the wonders and eccentricities of marriage make for some great material at a wedding.

Just remember to know your audience; make fun of yourself first if you're going to gently tease someone else; say some nice things along the way; and close with a tribute to the beneficiary of your toast.

Please note that I've chosen to intersperse the more earnest quotes and offers of advice with some humourous one-liners and wry observations about marriage. I've done that purposely, as I believe the best wedding speeches combine a sprinkling of laughter with a large measure of hope and goodwill. So here's to your success (and don't forget to check your fly).

May the twinkle in your eyes stay with you, and the love in your hearts never fade.

May the love you share forever remain as beautiful as the bride looks today.

Do not marry a person that you know you can live with; only marry someone that you cannot live without.

Love is blind, but marriage can be a real eye-opener.

A rhetorical question only a married man can appreciate: If a man stands alone in the forest, and there are no women around to hear him speak, is he still wrong?

No one in love is free, or wants to be.

The most important thing in a relationship between a man and a woman is that one of them must be good at taking orders.

Success is getting what you want. Happiness is wanting what you get.

Once married, remember that the length of a minute depends on which side of a bathroom door you're standing on.

The most effective way to remember your spouse's birthday is to forget it once.

Some people are so determined to find blissful happiness that they overlook a lifetime of contentment.

There are some who feel it is inappropriate to make fun of the holy institution of marriage. Then there are others who know it's the only way we can live with it.

A good marriage is like a casserole; only those responsible for it really know what goes in it.

My wife only has two complaints. One, she has nothing to wear. Two, there's never enough space in her closet.

Advice for newly-weds: A closed mouth carries no foot.

Marriage is the process of finding out what kind of person your spouse would have really preferred.

A husband is living proof that a wife can take a joke.

Number one tip for all newlyweds: your mother-in-law is always right (and she'll be the first to tell you that).

Love does not keep a ledger of the sins and failures of others.

Remember: On any disagreement, the husband is always entitled to the last few words ... "Yes, dear."

Always remember that a woman has the last word in any argument. Anything a man says after that ... is the beginning of a new argument.

I can only hope that you will be as happy in life as me and "What's her name?"

Keep your eyes open before marriage – half shut afterwards.

Let there be spaces in your togetherness.

Love is made visible by work.

Women are made to be loved, not to be understood.

It's usually better to be reasonable rather than right.

Life isn't a matter of milestones, but of moments.

Behind every successful man stands a woman – nagging, nagging, nagging.

Behind every successful man stands a woman – totally surprised.

Always remember that there are two theories to arguing with a woman. Neither one works.

Sometimes I wake up Grumpy. Other times I let him sleep.

A good wife and health – are a man's best wealth.

Love is the fountain from which all goodness flows.

Down the hatch, to a striking match!

Love is simply giving someone your undivided attention.

Married couples who love each other tell each other tell each other a thousand things without talking. (Chinese proverb)

Husbands seldom realize that when they say "I do" ... they *do* everything.

A woman marries a man expecting he will change, but he doesn't. A man marries a woman expecting that she won't change ... and she does.

Love will endure when you keep it pure.

New shoes, red wine & big diamond rings ... these are a few of my favorite things.

Any married man should forget his mistakes. There's no use in two people remembering the same thing.

If there is such a thing as a good marriage, it's because it more closely resembles friendship than romance.

I always "see" better with my heart.

Remember to always make the little decisions with your head and the big decisions with your heart.

May you both unite as a single soul dwelling in two bodies.

May you complete each other – and grow as one.

Remember that no matter how thin you slice it, there are always two sides.

Someone once said: "Criticism never built a house, wrote a play, composed a song, painted a picture or improved a marriage."

It is often because two people are so different from each other that they have so much to share.

Every woman has two husbands – the one she is given, and the one she creates.

Love is what makes two people sit in the middle of a bench when there's plenty of room at both ends.

I wish you both the time to celebrate the simple joys.

Forget the troubles that pass away. Give thanks for the blessings that pass your way.

May all your troubles be little ones.

Love the things you love for what they are.

The sweetest love is unconditional.

Love is nothing without friendship.

The more you love each other, the closer you will come to God.

There is nothing greater in life than to love another, and to be loved in return.

The surest way to be fully loved is to love fully.

Above all, remember this: Your love is the greatest gift you can possibly give each other.

The road to a long and successful marriage is called friendship.

Before marriage a man will lie awake all night thinking about something you said; after marriage, he'll fall fast asleep before you finish saying it.

If we take matrimony at its lowest form, we regard it as a sort of friendship recognized by the police.

God is the only third party in a marriage that can make it work.

The sea of matrimony is filled with hardships. Share them as one and you will both grow stronger and love more deeply.

A comment on the times: People do not marry as early as they used to, but they seem to marry more often.

If you want your wife to really listen to what you say, just talk in your sleep.

You only get married for the second time once.

Marriage is like a long meal to be slowly savoured together.

First thrive and then wive.

Equity and material success will never sustain a marriage. It's the equity you build in your hearts that's important.

A wise woman will always let her husband have her way.

The wedding march always reminds me of the music played when soldiers go to battle.

May you both look back on the past with as much pleasure as you look forward to the future.

May the bridge you build together span a lifetime.

May you share in the joy of building a home, raising children, growing old together and being blessed with grandchildren.

A good marriage is when you say, "How do I love thee, let me count the ways" – and you reach for a calculator.

Who are we kidding? A husband controls his wife like a barometer controls the weather!

You know the marriage didn't work out when the thank you notes for the presents are signed by a lawyer.

The great secret of a successful marriage is to treat all disasters as incidents and none of the incidents as disasters.

Generally the woman chooses the man who will choose her.

You think you have troubles. Two months ago my wife left me for good – and my mother-in-law didn't.

Often the difference between a successful marriage and a mediocre one consists of leaving about three or four things a day unsaid.

A sound marriage is not based on complete frankness; it is based on a sensible reticence.

Always remember that in the grammatically correct marriage, the bride says "I do" ... and the groom says, "I will."

Remember always: Love has no endings, only beginnings.

Love is only for the young ... the middle-aged ... and the old.

A hug is worth a thousand words.

A wedding wish: May you never forget what is worth remembering, or remember what is worth forgetting.

May you *truly* live all the days of your life together.

A happy marriage is a union of two forgivers.

My opinions are my own, and my wife says I'm darn lucky to have them.

You'd be amazed at how quickly a quiet apology, in word or deed, can return lost smiles and rekindle old passions.

My wife says if I go fishing one more time she's going to leave me. Gosh, I'm going to miss her.

Nuns have been described as women who marry God. So if they divorce Him, do they get half the universe?

Shotgun wedding: a case of wife or death.

The only one of your children who does not grow up and move away is your husband.

The theory used to be you marry an older man because they are more mature. The new theory is that men don't mature. So you might as well marry a younger one.

Bumper sticker: "No cash on premises. My wife has it all."

All marriages are happy – it's the living together afterward that causes all the problems.

May you be blessed with a wife so healthy and strong, she can pull the plow when your horse drops dead.

May you be blessed with a husband so worldly and wise that he knows the value of a closet full of shoes.

Sign in a marriage counselor's window: "Out to lunch – think it over."

Don't look for the perfect spouse in each other, try to be the perfect spouse for each other.

A good wife is God's smile from heaven.

Little surprises will keep your love exciting and fresh.

I had some words with my wife. She had some paragraphs with me.

A son asked his father, is it true that in some parts of Africa a man doesn't know his wife until he marries her? His father replied: That happens in most countries, son.

In times of trouble, flowers are a man's best friend.

When a newly married man looks happy we know why. But when a man married ten years or more looks happy – we wonder why.

Married life is very frustrating. In the first year of marriage, the man speaks and the woman listens. In the second year, the woman speaks and the man listens. In the third year, they both speak and the neighbors listen.

After a quarrel, a wife said to her husband, "You know, I was a fool when I married you." And the husband replied, "Yes, dear, but I was in love and didn't notice it."

It doesn't matter how often a married man changes his job, he still ends up with the same boss.

When a man opens the door of his car for his wife, you can be sure of one thing: Either the car or the wife is new.

A perfect wife is one who helps the husband with the dishes.

My wife and I were deliriously happy for 20 years. Then we met.

Marriage is a great institution – if in fact you're ready for an institution.

Marriage is the most expensive way to get your laundry done.

A health tip for newlyweds. Never, under any circumstances, take a sleeping pill and a laxative on the same night.

Advice for the groom: The two most important words for you to remember throughout your marriage are, "Yes, dear."

A husband is a person who is under the impression he bosses the house – when in reality, he only houses the boss.

Husbands are a lot like the government, they promise a lot more than they can deliver.

To speak frankly, I am not in favor of long engagements. They give people the opportunity of finding out about each other's character before marriage, which I think is never advisable.

I want to get as thin as my first husband's promises.

Marriage is when a man and woman become as one; the trouble starts when they try to decide which one.

Some people ask the secret of our long marriage. We take time to go to a restaurant two times a week. A little candlelight dinner, soft music and dancing. She goes Tuesdays, I go Fridays.

The worst reconciliation is preferable to the best divorce.

It begins with a prince kissing an angel. It ends with a baldheaded man looking across the table at a fat woman.

The average man lays down the law to his wife and then accepts all her amendments.

No married man ever pokes fun at a woman for shopping all day and buying nothing.

No woman can satisfactorily explain to herself why she married her husband.

May the garden of your life together be full and ripe and bountiful.

Being a husband is a lot like any other job. It helps if you like the boss.

May your friendship endure in both sunshine and shade.

May you share a joy that grows deeper, a friendship that grows closer, and a marriage that grows richer through the years.

My wife only has two complaints. One, she has nothing to wear. Two, there's never enough space in her closet.

Behind every unsuccessful man stands a woman – saying I told you so – and the mother agrees.

All men are born free, but some get married.

I must say, they do make a perfect couple. Except for him!

Being a husband is a lot like any other job. It helps if you like the boss.

Never speak loudly to each other – unless the house is on fire.

Success in marriage is more than finding the right person; it is the matter of being the right person.

A successful marriage is the result of falling in love often – with the same person.

Share your faith. Pray for each other in the morning. Pray together at night. And be together in spirit throughout each day.

Choose a wife rather by your ear than by your eye.

In the word wedding, the "we" comes before the "i."

Falling in love is an exquisite but complex coming together of two individuals. Marriage is the union of their souls.

I always have the last word with my wife – even if I have to go into another room to say it.

Like Thumper said: "If you can't say something nice, don't say nuthin' at all."

FAMOUS QUOTES ON MARRIAGE

Joy is not in things. It is in us. – Wagner

The time to be happy is now. The place to be happy is here. – Robert G. Ingersoll

Love is all you need. – Lennon/McCartney

Love cometh like sunshine after rain. – William Shakespeare

Love is to life what sunshine is to plants and flowers. – Tom Blandi

Love is not a matter of counting the years. It is making the years count. – William Smith

Love is what you go through together. – Thornton Wilder

Prescription for a happy marriage: Whenever you're wrong, admit it, whenever you're right, shut up. – Ogden Nash

Love must be learned, and learned again and again; there is no end to it. – Katherine Anne Porter

To love a person means to agree to grow old with them. – Albert Camus

The love we have in our youth is superficial compared to the love that an old man has for an old wife. – Will Durant

Once you have learned to love, you have learned to live. – Walter M. Germain

Love is an act of endless forgiveness, a tender look which becomes a habit. – Peter Ustinov

Never above you. Never below you. Always beside you. – Walter Winchell

Marriage is not a ceremony. It is a creation! – Charlie W. Shedd

There is no more lovely, friendly and charming relationship, communion or company than a good marriage. – Martin Luther

Sometimes the hardest thing you will have to do is endure to the end of the day. Sometimes life will be so grand that the day will seem too short. – Bernice Smith

You will truly know you are married when the bills start to come and you learn to share the toothpaste. – Bernice Smith

Remember that nothing is worth more than this day. – Goethe

Having it all doesn't necessarily mean having it all at once.
– Stephanie Luethkehans

Remember that women ... and elephants ... never forget.
– Dorothy Parker

I'm an excellent housekeeper. Every time I get a divorce, I keep the house. – Zsa Zsa Gabor

The heart that loves is always young. – Greek proverb

Never go to bed mad. Stay up and fight. – Phyllis Diller

Eighty percent of married men cheat in America. The rest cheat in Europe. – Jackie Mason

The great question ... which I have not been able to answer ... is, "What does a woman want?" – Freud

There's a way of transferring funds that is even faster than electronic banking. It's called marriage. – James Holt McGavran

Grow old along with me – the best is yet to be. – Robert Browning

Love is the flower that grows. – John Lennon

A successful marriage requires falling in love many times, always with the same person. – Mignon McLaughlin

Background on the Author

Tom Haibeck is a marketing and communications specialist who has helped plan (and spoken at) hundreds of events – including weddings, special events, conferences, press briefings and receptions.

He began his career in the communications industry as a radio newscaster and reporter. He later attended Simon Fraser University, where he graduated with a Bachelor of Arts degree, majoring in communications.

After university, Tom worked for several large advertising and public relations agencies before launching his own communications firm in 1988 (see **Haibeck.com**). Over the past 25+ years, he has provided media and speaker-training services to thousands of executives, community leaders and professional entertainers throughout North America.

Tom is a past president of the American Marketing Association, and is an accredited public relations professional (APR). He has served on numerous professional and community boards, and is a recipient of the highest award for achievent in the Dale Carnegie Training program.

Tom and his family live in the Pacific Northwest. His passions are writing, reading, movies, travel and sports (especially golf, tennis and hockey). For more background on Tom and his adventures as an emcee and toastmaster, please see his websites: **TheWeddingMCBook.com** and **WeddingToasts.com**.